£8·99.

WORKING FOR TH

Other How To Books

Applying for a Job
Budgeting for Students
Building Self-Esteem
Career Networking
Career Planning for Women
Controlling Anxiety
Critical Thinking for Students
Doing Voluntary Work Abroad
Finding a Job with a Future
Finding Work Overseas
Gaining a Master's Degree
Getting a Job After University
Getting a Place at University
Getting That Job
Going to University
How to Claim State Benefits
How to Find Temporary Work
  Abroad
How to Get a Job Abroad
How to Know Your Rights:
  Students
How to Manage Your Career
How to Market Yourself
How to Return to Work
How to Study Abroad
How to Study & Learn

How to Survive College
How to Work in an Office
Improving Your Written English
Learning New Job Skills
Living Away from Home
Making Decisions
Managing Projects
Making Work Experience Count
Managing Your First Computer
Managing Your Time
Managing Yourself
Maximising Your Memory
Passing Exams Without Anxiety
Passing That Interview
Planning a New Career
Planning Your Gap Year
Research Methods
Staying Ahead at Work
Studying at University
Studying for a Degree
Taking Your A-Levels
Unlocking Your Potential
Writing a CV that Works
Writing an Assignment
Writing an Essay
Writing Your Dissertation

Other titles in preparation

The How To series now contains nearly 250 titles in the following categories:

Business & Management
Computer Basics
General Reference
Jobs & Careers
Living & Working Abroad

Personal Finance
Self-Development
Small Business
Student Handbooks
Successful Writing

Please send for a free copy of the latest catalogue for full details (see back cover for address).

JOBS & CAREERS

WORKING FOR THE ENVIRONMENT

How to make a career of caring
for the world we live in

Barbara Buffton

How To Books

British Library Cataloguing in Publication Data
A catalogue record for this book is available from the British Library.

First published by How To Books Ltd, 3 Newtec Place,
Magdalen Road, Oxford, OX4 1RE, United Kingdom.
Tel: (01865) 793806. Fax: (01865) 248780.
email: info@howtobooks.co.uk
www.howtobooks.co.uk

Note: The material contained in this book is set out in good faith for
general guidance and no liability can be accepted for loss or expense
incurred as a result of relying in particular circumstances on statements
made in this book. The law and regulations may be complex and liable to change,
and readers should check the current position with the relevant authorities
before making personal arrangements.

Produced for How To Books by Deer Park Productions.
Typeset by Concept Communications (Design & Print) Ltd, Crayford, Kent.
Printed and bound by Cromwell Press, Trowbridge, Wiltshire.

Contents

List of Illustrations

Preface

This book explores the many opportunities that exist for anyone interested in making a career out of caring for the environment, whether you are a college student, a graduate, or someone looking for that first job or a change of career.

Increasing numbers of people, organisations and governments are now taking practical steps to be more environmentally responsible. One of the outcomes of this global concern is an increase in the number and range of environmental jobs and careers.

This book provides extensive up-to-date information about the huge (and sometimes confusing) variety of different career opportunities in the public, private, voluntary and statutory sectors. Whatever your interest in the environment, whether it is plants, animals, land, natural resources, pollution, waste disposal, health or environmental science, you will find useful information here about the nature of the work, the different posts and the type of employer as well as how to become skilled and qualified.

In addition, the book helps you identify which career area would most suit you, by providing practical self-assessment exercises aimed at evaluating your skills, interests and attributes. There are handy hints and tips to make yourself more employable and for getting that all-important first 'foot in the door'.

I would like to thank all the organisations mentioned in the book who checked the text and provided me with material, the people whose stories formed the basis of the case studies and Barry Mortimer, my long-suffering husband, whose critical appraisal and loving support are invaluable to me.

Barbara Buffton

1
Understanding the Environment

PUTTING IT ALL IN CONTEXT

'Air pollution is hastening the deaths of up to 24,000 people a year.'
'More than 70 per cent of motorists use their cars to travel less than one mile.'
'Height of waves increasing.'
'Green belt under threat.'

These recent extracts from newspapers highlight vividly how we are polluting and changing our environment. Although most people have heard of global warming and the thinning of the ozone layer, there is still much for us all to learn about the risks we are taking with our planet.

Land, air, freshwater and sea make up our environment and provide us with many diverse resources – minerals, oil, gas, water, plants and animals. Humans, animals and plants all depend on the natural environment to survive. The protection of the environment depends on the interaction, interrelation and interdependency between the physical, the biological and the human. For example, you cannot protect birds without protecting the habitat; you cannot protect the habitat without considering climate change, the effects of pesticides or soil erosion, and so on. This explains why work in the environmental field spans so many different areas.

Over the last two decades, people have become more conscious of the harm caused to the living world by humans.

> There is a growing awareness that if we do not take practical steps to look after our surroundings, and live in a more environmentally responsible way, we may not have a clean and healthy world to pass on to future generations.

Identifying the issues
The following issues are of particular concern:

11

● The effects of pollution on air, land, freshwater and the sea by chemicals, sewage and radioactivity.

● The exploitation of land use by mining and road building and the loss of green fields to housing developments.

● Climate change through production of the 'greenhouse gases' (thought to be caused largely by human activities).

● The loss of natural habitats and extinction of species through intensive farming, neglect, tourism, agricultural change, mineral extraction, pollution, etc.

● Waste management, for example through recycling and minimisation.

It is recognised that Western lifestyles do not contribute to the sustainable development of the environment, ie we take out more than can be replaced naturally. For example, one per cent of the world's population lives in the UK and yet we use two per cent of the planet's sustainable timber yield and almost five per cent of its sustainable steel and aluminium production. *Tomorrow's World*, a recent report from Friends of the Earth, states that we must reduce our consumption of resources drastically within the next 50 years if supplies of wood, water and metals are not to run out.

It can be seen, therefore, that there is plenty of scope for work in this area for anyone who is interested in contributing to the sustainability of the environment.

Improving the environment

Many organisations (voluntary, business, government) are supporting various initiatives to improve the environment, such as:

● restoring landscapes and wildlife habitats
● making positive use of wasteland in and around towns and cities
● protecting wildlife
● improving energy efficiency
● minimising waste
● reducing traffic.

In recent years, the threat to our planet from the over-exploitation of natural resources (for example, wood, freshwater and fish) and pollution has been taken seriously by many countries. Research into renewable energy sources, such as sun, wind, water and combustible waste, is just one example of how countries are responding to the dangers.

In the UK there have been radical changes in attitudes to the environment. These have resulted in practical steps to address the problems. For instance, there is now legislation which covers the level of car exhaust emissions, the treatment and disposal of water, the use of water and energy – for example, the Home Energy Conservation Act (1995) sets energy conservation targets for local authorities to meet.

To help comply with the various rules and regulations, and sometimes because of a genuine desire to protect or improve the environment, larger organisations have created environmental posts. The role of environmental staff is to monitor, assess and lessen the impact of their company's business on the environment.

Increasing political awareness

'Green' issues are now high on the political as well as the business agenda. Tony Blair has committed his Government to producing a draft green budget and promised that sustainable development will be at the heart of its policies.

In 1992, a major United Nations Conference on Environment and Development (the 'Earth Summit') met in Rio de Janeiro, Brazil. Leaders of 179 governments (including that of the UK) discussed how communities and individuals can take positive action to stop the depletion of the world's stock.

Local action

One of the effects of that world conference was the introduction of **Local Agenda 21** – how to encourage local authorities to take action at a local level, involving communities as well as business and voluntary organisations. The world's leaders agreed that our quality of life was being compromised by our unsustainable lifestyles. They therefore developed a plan to encourage cooperation and action at both global and local levels. It is not a statutory obligation and yet many local authorities (approximately 70 per cent) in the UK have already made a commitment to the Local Agenda 21 process.

Local Agenda 21 projects are as diverse as the local authorities and depend a great deal on which local issues are of greatest concern. For example, in rural areas the emphasis might be on protecting the countryside; in urban areas it might be on the regeneration of neglected sites. In all areas there will undoubtedly be concern about waste management and energy conservation. Whatever the issues, the role of local authority environmental coordinators or Local Agenda 21 officers is to encourage the council, the community and individuals to be as 'green' as possible.

Climate change
More recently, the 1997 Kyoto Climate Summit in Japan brought together many governments, scientists and pressure groups to consider global cooperation to correct the balance of the ecosystems threatened by the changes in climate. According to one newspaper report (*Guardian Education* 9.12.97), temperatures have risen by 0.6 degrees this century, with the eight warmest years (since global records began) being from 1988.

Debates took place on many different areas of environmental concern, including how to:

● reduce climate-altering emission levels of carbon dioxide
● promote renewable energy
● adapt economies and legislation for the protection of species and habitats in the rising temperatures
● and reduce pollution.

The way forward
Our natural resources are becoming depleted and pollution is harming the environment due to many factors, including:

● a growing human population
● an ever-increasing need for food and resources
● the heavy demand that the modern industrial society places on the environment.

It is therefore becoming increasingly obvious that we must learn to understand more about our environment, so that we can begin to:

● manage the earth's biological resources more wisely
● arrest adverse trends such as the thinning of the ozone layer and global warming
● ensure that we reach sustainable solutions to the environmental problems and challenges which we all face.

These concerns and issues, although obviously worrying, present opportunities for anyone interested in working in the environmental field.

GENERAL TRENDS

Increasing job opportunities

The growing concern for the environment has meant an increase in career opportunities in the environmental field both in the UK and abroad. Employment in industry is likely to increase as concern with environmental problems continues to grow.

The Organisation for Economic Cooperation and Development (OECD) estimates that the global market for environmental technology and services will soon overtake that for aerospace (*Green Futures*, magazine of Forum for the Future, Jan/Feb 1998). One reason for this is that countries with environmental problems, such as Southeast Asia with its recent problem of smog, are creating new markets for environmental jobs. The Department of Trade and Industry and the Department of the Environment, Transport and the Regions have responded to the demand by creating a Joint Environmental Markets Unit to help UK companies get a foothold in this global market.

Controlling waste and pollution

Recent laws on pollution and waste disposal have also led to an increase in jobs. Over 80,000 people now work in waste management and an increasing number of local authorities and other organisations are recruiting waste disposal managers, recycling officers and pollution control officers, as well as environmental coordinators.

Popularity of environmental courses

There is now a growing diversity of courses related to the environment, reflecting the popularity amongst students and possibly the increasing demand from employers. The courses vary tremendously in titles and content and are covered in more detail in a later chapter.

OUTLINING THE OPTIONS

In view of the complexity of issues surrounding the protection and improvement of the environment, there are many different areas of environmental work depending on where your interest lies. Some of the main ones are outlined below:

Plants and animals

Some people work with only plants, or with only animals; others work with both. Employment in this area may include the following:

- the active management and conservation of habitats
- monitoring the quality of all kinds of habitats, from tropical rainforests and heathlands to hedgerows and sewage outlets
- researching animal and plant behaviour; studying how plants and animals interact with their natural surroundings
- protecting wildlife
- assessing the impact of the environment on flora and fauna
- monitoring populations of endangered species; encouraging rare species to thrive.

Land

This area includes nature conservation, architecture, land management, surveying and town and country planning. Some of the opportunities include:

- identifying and protecting sites of special scientific interest
- managing parks, gardens, farms, nature reserves
- conservation of areas for public enjoyment
- keeping lands and roads clean
- planning and developing new habitats for wildlife
- assessing the environmental impact of new developments on land
- protecting the 'green belt' and countryside.

Natural resources

This is a growing area of concern, as natural resources become scarcer. Jobs include:

- conserving energy
- researching renewable energy resources
- regulating the use of natural resources (making policy and ensuring good practice)
- planning the use of major resources such as water
- recycling and recovering materials and household and industrial waste
- promoting energy efficiency.

Pollution and waste disposal

People working in these areas are concerned with ensuring that the environment is as clean and as healthy as possible. The opportunities are varied and include:

- researching and developing waste disposal methods

- monitoring and processing sewage and waste disposal
- investigating soil and water contamination
- controlling and monitoring the quality of water
- carrying out pollution prevention inspections
- managing landfill sites
- handling local government waste collection.

Health

This generally concerns the health of people both at home and at work. Employment options include:

- inspecting food premises
- investigating unhygienic housing conditions
- checking on health and safety standards at work
- enforcing laws regarding pollution (air, noise, land).

Other areas

As can be seen, some areas overlap, reinforcing the belief that all things environmental are necessarily interrelated! In addition to the opportunities outlined above, there is also limited scope for working in the environmental science field, for example studying population biology, meteorology, climatology or oceanography.

IDENTIFYING THE JOBS

Many different organisations, in the private, public and voluntary sectors, employ scientists and technologists. The jobs may be in scientific research, assessment, monitoring or consultancy. However, you do not have to be scientifically- or technically-minded to take part in protecting or conserving the environment.

Different needs

Organisations need a whole range of other people to complement and support the work of professionals more directly involved in the practical field and laboratory work. For instance, there may be opportunities for librarians, photographers, engineers, public relations specialists, cartographers, administrators, accountants, personnel officers and secretaries in environmental organisations or in local and central government environmental departments.

It may be that you gain professional qualifications in another area before becoming involved or interested in environmental work. Some jobs make it possible to combine the two, such as journalism or teaching. It is very important to educate the public about the threat to the environment. Public relations people in environmental organisations are also needed to inform the public and future generations about the environment. They may do this by sending out information, taking part in science exhibitions and initiatives or in public awareness campaigns.

Different levels

The range of work is wide and the qualifications required are variable, depending on the type of job. As in many other career options, it is possible to leave school at 16 and get a job or go on to further and higher education. For example, in conservation work, there are opportunities for:

● estate workers (mending fences, digging ditches, building walls, etc) with few or no qualifications
● conservation wardens (often now called site managers) who come from a variety of backgrounds
● conservation officers who may be scientific officers with degree-level qualifications
● countryside managers who may have relevant degrees (agriculture, geology, geography, environmental science, etc) or relevant experience, such as a background in farming or surveying.

Some posts may also require postgraduate qualifications in conservation, ecology or land management.

So if you really are concerned about the environment, there may be a post for you, whatever your qualifications, skills or interests. It is safe to say, however, that the more qualifications you have, the more options there will be open to you.

CHECKLIST

1. Look through newspapers and listen to the news. What can you learn about the environment?

2. What environmental issues are important where you live? Is waste disposal the main problem, or development of land, or something else?

3. How serious are you about concern for the environment? For example, how much of your household waste is recycled?

4. What voluntary organisations can you name which are concerned with protecting the environment?

5. Is your local authority involved in Local Agenda 21? If so, what initiatives are they introducing?

6. Which environmental areas most interest you at the moment?

7. Which level and type of job are you aiming for?

CONSIDERING A CAREER IN THE ENVIRONMENT

What to think about when considering a career in this area:

Advantages

- There are many different areas to choose from.
- It is possible to work for an environmental organisation without having an environmental qualification.
- There is no one direct route to an environmental career.
- You are helping to conserve the environment for future generations.

Disadvantages

- You might find it difficult to find out where your interests lie.
- You may need a lot of voluntary experience before finding a job.
- Many of the jobs demand degree-level qualifications.
- Some of the work (for example, consultancy) may be short-term.

DISCUSSION POINTS

1. What is the point of Local Agenda 21? How does it protect or improve the environment?

2. There are many different areas of environmental work. How could you decide which one interests you?

3. Why do you think concern for the environment is growing?

2
Working in the Public Sector

This chapter covers environmentally related jobs within the public sector – in local authorities, central government, the Forestry Commission and in publicly accountable bodies such as the Environment Agency and the Natural Environment Research Council.

WORKING FOR LOCAL GOVERNMENT

Local authorities are large employers – in total they employ over two million people in England and Wales (one in nine of the workforce) in a wide variety of different occupations. As a local government officer, you may find yourself working for a:

- county or district council (spread throughout England)
- metropolitan district or city council (spread throughout England)
- London borough
- unitary authority (Wales and Scotland, and parts of England)
- the Corporation of London (a unique unitary authority serving a geographical area of one square mile).

If you want to serve your local community and work for the environment, then local government may have the job for you. Local authorities are becoming more concerned with protecting and conserving the environment and therefore job opportunities in this area are increasing. In fact, there are probably more opportunities for working in environmental services within local authorities than there are anywhere else currently.

An increasing number of services that used to be operated by local authority staff, such as waste disposal and refuse collection, are now often carried out by private contractors. However, local authorities are still major employers. For instance, out of 80,000 people employed in the waste management industry, 50,000 are employed in the local authority sector.

Flexible working

Local authorities are renowned for having introduced a range of flexible working arrangements, such as flexitime (flexible starting and finishing times), job shares, part-time, term-time and annual-hours contracts (where the period worked is defined over a whole year according to need). It may also be possible to negotiate career breaks, paid sabbaticals, secondments or remote working (tele-working or home working).

Employment opportunities

There is usually no one department within a local authority with exclusive responsibility for looking after the environment. This is because the range of posts concerned with the environment is so wide. Some of the more obvious environmentally related jobs include the following:

● Overseeing the recycling and disposal of waste (for example, waste management officer, waste disposal officer, recycling officer).

● Making the best use of land and its natural resources (for example, town and country planner, planner).

● Protecting the environment (for example, countryside manager/warden/ranger, environmental manager/coordinator).

● Creating safe and pleasant environments for people to live and work in (for example, landscape architect, architect).

● Ensuring health standards are maintained (for example, environmental health officer).

● Developing and agreeing local policies for sustainable development of the environment (for example, environmental manager/coordinator, Local Agenda 21 officer).

Many other local government jobs not mentioned above could also be said to have an environmental aspect to them. For example, housing officers, parks maintenance staff, engineers and surveyors take into account the effects of their work on the environment and have to be sensitive to environmental issues.

Typical duties

Although responsibilities vary greatly and will differ depending on the job and the authority, most of the posts below will involve one or more of the duties outlined. In addition, many local government officer posts involve close liaison with other professionals and experts, offering specialist support, knowledge and advice. Local authorities encourage a multi-disciplinary approach to problem-solving.

Waste management

Waste management and waste disposal officers manage the collection, recycling, disposal and regulation of waste. Their responsibilities may include the disposal of household waste, choosing landfill sites and overseeing the transport of waste.

Recycling officers promote waste minimisation and recycling both in-house and with the public. Their work may involve visiting recycling sites, checking on the work of contractors and ensuring sites are clean. They have to develop good relations with the press to publicise any new initiatives such as the recycling of paper, glass, cans, textiles and plastic bottles.

Town and country planning

Town and country planners help to preserve and improve the environment in their role as developers of urban and rural areas. They are concerned with the needs of both community and business and may also contribute to local authority policy planning.

A major part of their work involves processing planning applications. For this, they have to make site inspections, consult with various interested bodies and other professionals (for example, surveyors, lawyers, architects, designers), write reports and make recommendations to the planning committee.

At all times they take into account the effects and implications of proposals on conservation, the environment and the local community.

Countryside management

The roles and duties of countryside managers, wardens and rangers often overlap and depend very much on the local authority concerned. Whatever the title, the work involves the physical management and protection of a geographical area (countryside parks, areas of outstanding natural beauty, woodlands, forests) and monitoring and protecting the quality of the natural environment.

Duties are varied and may include carrying out site inspections, educating the public, organising events for the public and managing visitors (helping people to enjoy the facilities without damaging the area) and visitor centres.

Environmental management

Environmental coordinators/managers (they may also be called project managers) set up and supervise the protection and conservation of the natural environment. Roles vary according to the needs of the local authority. However, some posts may involve improving the wildlife in urban areas, and creating nature conservation and recreation strategies for towns and cities; others may involve ensuring that all aspects of an authority's work take environmental awareness and policy into consideration.

Landscape architecture

Landscape architects work closely with architects and planners. Basically their role is to design the outdoor environment, ensuring that it meets the needs of urban and rural communities. Some of their work may involve rehabilitation – improving existing landscapes (for example, car parks, parks, woodlands, pedestrian zones, grounds or spaces around public buildings).

Local Agenda 21 officers

The role of these officers is to encourage the authority, the community and individuals to be as 'green' as possible, adopting strategies at local levels. Sometimes environmental coordinators or managers take on this role, at other times local authorities may create specific Local Agenda 21 Officer posts. (See Chapter 1 for further information on Local Agenda 21.)

The work includes developing and agreeing local policies for sustainable development of the environment. They spend time liaising with the different local authority departments to promote awareness of environmental issues. It is also important to encourage public participation in environmentally friendly projects such as recycling, by building relationships and partnerships between education, business and the wider community.

Environmental health officers

Environmental health officers (EHOs) are unlike the other posts in that they do not have direct involvement with protecting or conserving the environment. They are, however, included here as their role is to protect the public from environmental health risks. Much of their time is spent advising people on how to improve the environment and reduce pollution. A major part of their role is to enforce legislation on food handling, health and safety, hygiene, infectious disease, water supplies, air and noise pollution.

They also deal with many complaints and enquiries ranging from the effects of contaminated land and water pollution to noise, dog fouling and the handling of food. EHOs take time out of the office to inspect and monitor business premises, taking samples (for example of food, soil, water) or measuring air, noise and water quality. Writing reports on their findings is another aspect of their work. Sometimes, when complaints or investigations lead to prosecution, officers have to give evidence in court.

Technicians/support staff

Throughout their work, local government officers are supported by technicians or support staff. They provide wide-ranging support, such as interpreting and collating statistics, research information, carrying out surveys and maintaining and storing information. Their work may also include preparing plans and using information and computer systems.

WORKING FOR CENTRAL GOVERNMENT

Central government sets out the objectives and legislation for the operation of environmental services. Many of the environmentally related jobs are therefore at policy level (developing and deciding policy, reporting to ministers) in government research institutes, the Department of the Environment, Transport and the Regions (DETR), the Department for International Development or in the Ministry of Agriculture, Fisheries and Food (MAFF). Advisory posts generally require a degree qualification and many years' practical experience of consultancy work in a relevant field.

Policy issues

As a result of the 1994 Second European Health Conference on the Environment and Health, the DETR has a National Environmental Health Action Plan (NEHAP) for improving the UK's environmental health. The NEHAP covers a wide variety of initiatives including:

● reducing levels of pollutants in air and drinking water
● improving the quality of bathing water
● reducing vehicle emissions (a major contributor to poor air quality)
● encouraging the responsible use of pesticides in agriculture
● promoting sustainable forestry.

Scientists carry out research and development on environmental issues such as the above on behalf of the government. There are many other research projects involving a range of issues from identifying environmental health hazards and evaluating ways of environmental accounting (placing an economic value on any damage caused) to measuring the effects of noise on health.

Any actions required as a result of the research are then carried out mainly at local level through local government, the Environment Agency or other government departments.

Other opportunities

Meteorology
There may also be opportunities for meteorologists with the Meteorological Office, one of the UK Civil Service agencies. Information can be obtained from the Capita Recruitment and Assessment Services, Innovation Court, New Street, Basingstoke, Hampshire RG21 7JB. Tel: (01256) 468551. Fax: (01256) 383785.

The Armed Forces
There may be opportunities in the Royal Army Medical Corps and the RAF as both employ environmental health technicians.

WORKING FOR THE FORESTRY COMMISSION

Did you know that woodland covers one tenth of Britain, with the largest percentage in Scotland? The Forestry Commission manages 35 per cent of it (over two million acres), with the rest owned by farmers (20 per cent), other private owners (35 per cent) and by public and voluntary bodies (ten per cent). Forests are important for many reasons, including the supply of wood and the provision of habitats for wildlife and conservation. They also help prevent global warming, by absorbing some of the carbon dioxide from the atmosphere.

Although the Forestry Commission is a government department and the conditions of employment match those of the Civil Service, its staff are not members of the Home Civil Service.

How the Commission works
The Commission's role is 'to protect and expand Britain's forests and woodlands and increase their value to society and the environment.' Three distinct sub-divisions carry out its objectives:

1. The Forestry Authority
This division deals with the various grants and licences for forestry work, regulations and control over forestry, research and advice on land uses.

2. Forest Enterprise
This is the agency responsible for the management and protection of the forests and woodlands throughout Great Britain.

3. The Policy and Resources Group
Based at the Commission's headquarters in Edinburgh, this division takes on the responsibility for the parliamentary and policy aspects. It also provides the personnel and business systems necessary for the operation of the other two sub-divisions.

No matter which division you work in, you will still be an employee of the Forestry Commission.

Type of work

The Commission's scope is therefore vast. A few of the many initiatives and projects it is involved in are listed below, to give some idea of the range:

- using derelict land to create new community forests
- converting former colliery spoil heaps (industrial wasteland) into landscaped multi-purpose woodlands
- conserving key species and habitats
- managing sites of special scientific interest.

Employment opportunities

The Forestry Commission offers many varied opportunities throughout Great Britain at all levels, from practical forestry work (forest officers, forest workers), landscape architecture, scientific and engineering work to land agency, conservation (rangers), administration and technical support.

WORKING FOR THE ENVIRONMENT AGENCY

The Environment Agency for England and Wales was established in 1996 and has taken over the functions of what used to be:

- the National Rivers Authority
- Her Majesty's Inspectorate of Pollution and
- the local authority run Waste Regulation Authorities.

By merging all these functions, the Environment Agency is able to oversee the protection and management of the whole environment – land, air and water.

Scotland

The Scottish Environment Protection Agency (SEPA) carries out similar functions, preventing pollution and protecting the environment in Scotland. It has combined the expertise of the former River Purification Boards, Her Majesty's Industrial Pollution Inspectorate and the waste regulation and air pollution powers held by Scotland's district and islands' councils. SEPA's remit for environmental protection and regulation in Scotland does not cover conservation, land use and water supply.

Northern Ireland

In Northern Ireland, the Environment and Heritage Service has responsibility for developing and implementing environmental policy. Its remit is the protection and conservation of the natural environment and the built heritage, and the protection of the environment from the pollution of air, water and land. As such it has very similar functions to the Environment Agency.

Employment opportunities

Employment opportunities for this kind of work in Wales and Northern Ireland are representative of those offered by the Environment Agency (see below). Although SEPA in Scotland also has a number of similar opportunities for work, its remit does not cover conservation, land use or water areas. Typical vacancies within SEPA might be for environmental protection officers, special waste coordinators or marine scientists.

There are employment opportunities in six main areas with the Environment Agency:

1. Environmental strategy

This section consists of various smaller divisions, employing environmental scientists, engineers and chemists who all work to increase general awareness of environmental issues. Their role involves strategic planning and project management and demands previous experience.

2. Flood defence

Flood defence teams comprise engineers, project managers and technicians. They are responsible for our sea and river defences with the aim first and foremost of protecting people and property from floods. This means not only constructing and maintaining defences, but also advising planning authorities and developers on flood risk and drainage. Engineers and hydrologists help identify areas of risk. It is of course a vital part of the team's role to take into account the environmental impact of each project.

When floods occur, the team has to deal practically with the situation and ensure that everyone involved is aware of the dangers.

3. Water resources
Hydrologists, hydrometric officers and hydrogeologists are just some of the professionals needed to manage the country's water resources. Hydrologists measure river flows, groundwater and rainfall levels. They gather information and analyse field data in order to predict future water supplies. Although they are mostly office-based, they do spend some time in the field testing and surveying.

Hydrometric officers and hydrogeologists measure water cycles of rivers and tributaries. They use the data collected to predict when rivers might flood. The role of hydrogeologists is also to assess the consequences of water pollution.

4. Pollution prevention and control
This section aims to prevent or control pollution. It employs a variety of professionals, including pollution control officers/inspectors, water quality planners and waste regulation officers. The members of the pollution control team 'prevent, minimise or render harmless' polluting substances into the environment, including radioactive materials.

Water quality staff are specifically involved with preventing water pollution, protecting rivers, estuaries, watercourses and the sea. They identify the source of any pollution, taking samples and readings.

A major role of all staff in this section is undertaking pollution prevention inspections in all manner of businesses, from farms and oil refineries to sewage works. They also have an advisory role with planners and local authorities. Some staff also deal with press and media publicity when pollution incidents occur.

5. Fisheries, recreation, conservation and navigation
Most regions have fisheries officers, some regions have conservation posts; others combine the posts of recreation, conservation and navigation.

The work in the Fisheries function of this section involves a mixture of laboratory and field work. Staff maintain, monitor and improve fish populations. They liaise with river users and landowners to prevent pollution affecting fish stocks.

The Recreation team manages sites and facilities for recreation use. These include rivers and lakes for angling, sailing and boating, and other water-related activities as well as pathways and facilities for cycling and horse-riding.

Staff in the Conservation function are involved in a wide range of different work including survey work, protecting the landscape and wildlife, liaising with other environmental organisations and advising other colleagues on the environmental impact of the Agency's own operations.

Navigation staff are responsible for managing and improving our inland waterways. The work varies from, for instance, maintaining or constructing locks and moorings to enforcing byelaws and dealing with navigation incidents.

6. Business support services
This section provides support for all the Environment Agency's activities. It employs a variety of staff, including scientists and technicians for work in the laboratories and in research and development, accountants, solicitors, planners, project managers, information services staff, press and publicity officers, education officers, personnel staff and training administrators.

WORKING FOR THE NATURAL ENVIRONMENT RESEARCH COUNCIL

The Natural Environment Research Council (NERC) is the leading body in the UK for environmental research, surveys, monitoring and training in all the environmental sciences. Its aim is to 'generate knowledge and understanding of the natural environment and to develop technologies and skills to apply that knowledge.'

It works in partnership with government, industry and other interested bodies, carrying out a broad range of activities including geological surveys, studies of the ocean and terrestrial ecology and the study of atmospheric, earth and life sciences.

The nature of the work
NERC has identified five principal environmental and natural resource issues in the UK:

● Biodiversity: understanding the vast and diverse array of habitats and associated plant and animal species that are important to our environment.

● Environmental risks and hazards: assessing and predicting natural disasters such as storms, floods, droughts, earthquakes and volcanic eruptions, and other potential hazards.

● Global change: understanding and predicting the impacts and implications of global change.

● Natural resources management: protecting the environment by managing coastal areas, improving the urban environment, surveying and managing sources of oil, gas, water and raw materials.

● Pollution: assessing and minimising its effects; and waste management: assessing methods of disposal of rubbish, dealing with contaminated land.

Scientists are providing the knowledge needed to respond to these challenges; their role is to understand the implications of the above major issues for conservation and environmental sustainability strategies.

Employment opportunities

There are opportunities for scientists, engineers and technologists from a broad range of disciplines to carry out field and laboratory work both in the UK and abroad. As with any large organisation, staff are also required for administrative, clerical, personnel, public relations and financial posts. In addition, because of the nature of some of the work, photographers, ship crews, radio operators, cooks, librarians and cartographers are also needed.

Not all of the work is global, much is at a local or national level. NERC employs nearly 3,000 people at 30 locations, including universities, a network of UK laboratories and five Centres and Surveys:

1. Southampton Oceanography Centre
2. Centre for Coastal and Marine Sciences
3. Centre for Ecology and Hydrology
4. British Antarctic Survey
5. British Geological Survey.

WORKING IN EDUCATION AND TRAINING

If you have an interest in protecting and conserving the environment and want to take the environmental message to more people, then a career in education and training might be the way forward. Teaching (primary, secondary or further education) offers many opportunities. For example, teaching subjects such as biology or geography. There is also the option of lecturing in higher education, depending on your level of qualification and the age range you want to teach. Lecturers are required in a variety of disciplines as diverse as ecology, environmental sciences, applied earth science and agricultural, food and environmental chemistry.

Public agencies and government research institutes advertise for information, publicity or education officers to help people who want to learn more about the environment and the organisation's role in protecting and conserving it. Staff in these posts work with the general public, local schools, colleges and universities, explaining the organisation's activities and often carrying out joint environmental projects. For example, NERC has a Schools Liaison Network and the Environment Agency has many staff in different roles who communicate its role in the environment.

The first green cybercafé

A good example of bringing green issues to the attention of the public is the opening of the world's first 'green' cybercafé in June 1998 in Cardiff. It is the result of a partnership between three organisations, including the county council. Its aim is to focus on one environmental topic a month, using the Internet to gather information and promote discussion. Green politics had a hand in this – a proportion of the café's development costs were funded by the landfill tax. (The *Times*, 17 June 1998.)

ENTRY AND QUALIFICATIONS

Specific qualifications required for public sector jobs vary from region to region and from post to post.

Relevant degrees

Many jobs and careers working with the environment require a degree in a related subject. Subjects directly relevant to environmental work, depending on your particular area of interest, could include:

● environmental science (natural environment)
● environmental studies (human, built environment)
● science (chemistry, physics, biology)
● ecology
● forestry
● geology

- hydrogeology/hydrology
- engineering (flood defence)
- oceanography
- geography
- environmental health
- chemical engineering (useful for waste disposal management or pollution control)
- meteorology
- countryside management and agriculture (useful for nature conservation posts)
- town planning
- landscape architecture.

Relevant A levels
Much of the work has a scientific bias and therefore science A levels or equivalent are usually required. Other useful subjects include economics and geography.

Environmental science A level is not always acceptable for science degrees. Check with university admissions tutors before committing yourself.

Postgraduate qualifications
Sometimes a Master's degree is preferred and it is often necessary to follow a first degree with postgraduate study to obtain professional status. For example, students with a first degree in science need a postgraduate degree in environmental health to become environmental health officers.

Work-related qualifications
In addition to GCSEs/SCEs, A and AS levels/Highers, there may be relevant NVQs/SVQs, GNVQs/GSVQs and BTEC or City and Guilds qualifications, such as the following:

- NVQs/SVQs at various levels in environmental conservation, agriculture, forestry, water services operations and distribution.

- Intermediate and Advanced GNVQs in Land and Environment (England and Wales) and GSVQs levels II and III in Land Based Industries (Scotland).

- BTEC national awards in agriculture, forestry.

Modern apprenticeships and national traineeships may also be available in your area, although at the time of writing national trainee-ships in environmental conservation are not yet offered in Scotland. This is only a sample of the many qualifications available. Check with your local college or careers service company for which ones are on offer in your area. All of these qualifications can lead to higher education or employment related to environmental services.

Specific public sector information

Local government
Posts for technicians and technical support staff generally require a minimum of four GCSEs (A-C) including maths. Many have A levels or equivalent on entry. Training is usually on the job, often combined with study towards professional qualifications.

The local government student sponsorship scheme offers paid work experience to a small number of higher education students who are committed to the idea of working for a local authority. The scheme gives them the opportunity to spend a minimum of five weeks with a local authority in the summer holidays prior to their final year. Details are available from the Local Government Management Board (see Useful Addresses, page 131).

Professional staff enter with a relevant degree or diploma. For example, environmental coordinators/managers may have a degree in environmental sciences, and town and country planners a degree in architecture, geography, economics, geology, statistics or town planning. Many work towards postgraduate or professional examinations while in post, such as those of the Chartered Institute of Environmental Health or the Royal Town Planning Institute. Most authorities contribute towards training costs and allow time off for attendance at college on a day or block release basis.

The Meteorology Office
Environmental science as a degree may be accepted if applicants have a good grounding in maths and physics. Relevant degrees include meteorology, mathematics, physics or computing.

The Armed Forces
Environmental health technicians require a minimum of five GCSEs (A-C) in English, maths, biology (or human biology), chemistry and physics.

The Forestry Commission
Vacancies for forest workers are filled through an annual competition

which is advertised in the national press and involves interviews usually held around May.

The Environment Agency
At the present time the Environment Agency does not operate a graduate recruitment scheme or student sponsorship.

The Natural Environment Research Council
Graduates require first degrees (generally upper second or better) and postgraduate qualifications relevant to their particular area of interest. Scientific support posts require a minimum of four GCSEs (A-C) including science and maths. Engineering and technical support posts require appropriate technical qualifications and experience.

Education and training
A relevant degree (for example, in science, geography, ecology) would give you a good background from which to teach at primary or secondary level.

Generally applicants for lecturing posts have a research degree (PhD) in addition to their first degree.

CASE STUDIES

Conserving the countryside
Ailsa became interested in nature conservation in her teens when she went with friends on a conservation working holiday. After doing Highers in biology, geography, English and chemistry she decided to take a year out and joined the Scottish division of the British Trust for Conservation Volunteers as a Volunteer Officer. This helped her make up her mind about what she really enjoyed doing. She went on to do a degree in conservation management which gave her practical work experience in countryside management. She is now working as a conservation officer for a local authority.

Controlling pollution
Matt took A levels in economics, biology and geography. As he had always been interested in 'green' issues, a careers adviser suggested environmentally related degrees. A BSc in environmental geography seemed to combine all his interests. The course he chose has a module on river management, which made him very aware of the impact on the environment of pollutants. In his first job as an assistant pollution control officer with the Environment Agency, his main role is to check that

firms are not going over the limits for discharging effluent to the rivers. He is considering doing a postgraduate environmental pollution science course via day release and hopes to be promoted to pollution officer before too long.

Working towards change on a local level

Naomi's Highers (biology, chemistry, geography, French, English, maths) and Sixth Year studies in geography and biology prepared her for a BSc degree in biology and ecology. Outside of her studies, she had various summer jobs and short-term environmentally related contract work (for example, setting up conservation resources on a local estate). Her interest in Local Agenda 21 work began during her postgraduate studies (MSc in environmental management). She was curious about how to achieve change at a local level. Her thesis was on Scottish Local Agenda 21 schemes.

Naomi made a lot of local authority contacts while working on her thesis and through these she learnt of many job opportunities, including her present position. Her work involves liaising with groups of volunteers and local councillors as well as other departments within the local authority, with the aim of looking at ways to encourage the council, the community and individuals to be as 'green' as possible.

She is currently involved in the coordination and planning for an event which challenges people to consider environmental issues in terms of what kind of future they can expect – a dream or a nightmare?

CONSIDERING PUBLIC SECTOR EMPLOYMENT

What to think about when considering a career in this area:

Advantages

- You serve your community as well as care for the environment.
- Local government has flexible working arrangements.
- Local authorities are large employers of staff.
- Depending on your role, your range of responsibilities might be wider than they would be in the private sector.
- Local authorities are keen to help staff develop new skills and responsibilities.
- The working hours tend to be more regular than may be the case in some private sector jobs.
- Depending on the role, there may be the opportunity to work directly with politicians and influence policy issues.

Environment Protection Officer

Joining one of our teams, you will be responsible for the regulation and enforcement of legislation controlling discharges to air and water, the storage, treatment and disposal of waste, and the use and disposal of sealed radioactive sources.

A dedicated Environment Protection Officer with proven ability to communicate our message to industrial operators, the agricultural community and the general public, you will be clear, authoritative and balanced in your approach.

Applicants should possess either an environmental degree with one year's experience in a pollution control post or a relevant science degree with three years' relevant work experience. You should ideally have (or be working towards) a relevant professional qualification. Knowledge of current environmental legislation is required.

Team Leaders – Conservation

You are an experienced conservationist who can deliver effective conservation strategies. You already know what our aims and objectives are. Excellent communication and interpersonal skills are just some of your many attributes.

We are looking for individuals with a broad based experience of conservation work, with a particular focus on rivers and wetlands. You will need a comprehensive knowledge of the planning and authorisation process and a clear understanding of the benefits which can be achieved through collaboration.

You'll need to be a graduate or equivalent with at least 5 years' relevant conservation experience.

Environmental Services Technical Officers

Whether you're a recent school leaver, a graduate or have relevant highways, transportation or civil engineering experience, we have vacancies right across the Transportation department. You'll have plenty of opportunity to develop your skills through cross-training within a variety of areas from highways to drainage, and if you want to work towards some formal qualifications, we'll give you all the encouragement you need.

Fig. 1. Examples of typical public sector vacancies.

Disadvantages

- Sources of employment are limited to local authorities, central government and its agencies.
- It is possible that you could earn more in the private sector than in the public sector.
- Competition can be keen for local authority environmentally related jobs.
- Some jobs involve time away from home (for example, with the NERC Survey units – British Antarctic Survey or British Geological Survey).
- Previous work experience is often required for graduate-level posts.

CHECKLIST

1. Does any of the public sector areas take your interest at the moment? Write down which ones and why.

2. How do you think working in the public sector differs from working in the private sector?

3. Consider which subjects you need to study for your chosen area(s).

4. Ask your careers adviser, family or friends if they know of someone doing the job in which you are interested. Talk to this person and find out what it's really like.

5. Contact the various organisations for up-to-date information about employment opportunities (see Useful Addresses for contact details).

6. What are the roles and responsibilities of the various environment protection agencies in the UK?

3
Working in the Private Sector

FINDING OUT WHO THE EMPLOYERS ARE

This chapter concentrates on the private sector opportunities for people wishing to combine concern for the environment with a career. Many of the jobs mentioned are also available in the public sector (see chapter 2). It is also important to remember that environmental organisations also employ staff in non-environmental posts, such as personnel, administration, media, public relations, accountancy, legal and so on. There may also be some opportunity for journalists to cover environmental issues or for environmentalists to become involved in media broadcasting or presenting. This section concentrates on specific environmental posts.

Increasing awareness

According to **Lantra**, the environmental training organisation (see Useful Addresses), most large and medium-sized companies employ environmental managers. More and more industrial and commercial companies are introducing environmental awareness and planning into their operations. They are appointing environmental managers to protect and implement their company's environmental policies. Employers range from huge multi-nationals to small private consultancies.

Government policy is that firms should be encouraged to put the environment on their business agenda and work towards conserving and protecting it as far as is possible. For example, some of the government plans and targets for industry include:

● reducing emissions of pollutants, for example from power stations
● using energy more effectively
● increasing the proportion of renewable energy sources.

The risks to health and to the sustainablility of the environment and our natural resources are the motivating factors to meet these and other such targets.

Both green and good
Caring for the environment can also be a good marketing opportunity for companies. For instance, using recycled paper or environmentally friendly packaging can often enhance a company's image, no matter what their product might be. A major retailer may have won more customers when it committed to using the railway network to transport its goods, in an effort to curb environmental pollution. Some people prefer to invest their money in banks and other financial organisations which deal in ethical, environmental or ecological investments.

> **There are many reasons for private sector organisations to become more environmentally aware – which can only increase employment prospects in this field.**

The employers

Looking through the vacancy pages of newspapers (particularly *The Guardian* on Wednesdays and *The Independent*) and specialist environmental or scientific journals (such as *The New Scientist* or *Nature*), it is easy to spot the main private sector employers. They include the following industries:

- oil, gas, electricity, petrochemical
- mining and exploration
- water
- food
- hotel
- retail
- financial
- waste management
- agrochemicals
- forestry
- construction.

FINDING OUT WHAT THE JOBS ARE

Many companies now employ environmental staff whose job titles vary from environmental managers or coordinators to environmental affairs specialists. Their role may be a generalist one, such as defining and ensuring the implementation of an effective environmental strategy and action plan for the company. On the other hand, companies may require someone with a more specialist role, such as the following:

Environmental impact assessment

Companies need to assess and monitor the impact of their activities on the environment. Environmental impact assessment is a procedure and management technique which analyses the predicted likely effects of proposed new developments on the environment. New developments include waste disposal or chemical installations (dealing with toxic or dangerous wastes), motorways, shops, towns and factories. It requires knowledge of a wide range of disciplines, such as planning, socio-economics, business economics, environmental policy and law, as well as relevant specialist field knowledge (for example construction, water resource management, land survey techniques).

Pollution control and waste management

Did you know that about 500 million tonnes of waste are produced each year in the UK? The government states that 'waste should only be incinerated or disposed of in landfills as a last resort'. Companies therefore need advice on how to manage their waste and keep their operations as environmentally friendly as possible.

Any company whose operations might have a detrimental effect on the environment may employ pollution control or waste management officers (see further information on these posts in Chapter 2). This is particularly important given the principle of 'the polluter pays'. No company wants to pay unnecessarily, as the fines can be crippling. Major employers include waste management companies, the utility (water, electricity, gas) companies and oil and petrochemical companies.

Environmental health

Chapter 2 described the role and function of environmental health officers (EHOs), the majority of whom work in the public sector. The more obvious employers in the private sector include food manufacturers and hotel and retail chains. Some EHOs work as consultants in industry and commerce, advising companies on issues such as health and safety, food hygiene, pollution control and the assessment of hazards.

Enviromental accounting

Some industries, for instance chemical and oil, incur environmental liability costs because of regulations and laws relating to pollution and waste disposal. They are likely to employ accounting staff specifically to identify the costs involved. These costs may relate to:

- monitoring emissions
- obtaining permits (for example, for discharging oil)
- special insurance fees
- potential fines and charges for non-compliance to regulations
- running an environmental department.

It is not only industrial companies which have to consider the costs of ensuring that their operations are environmentally friendly, but also companies within the service industry. For example, financial organisations employ staff to consider the costs and implications involved in environmental investments and funds.

Environmental law

Lawyers specialising in planning or property law may also deal with environmental litigation. However, it is now becoming a specialism in its own right. Some major law firms have environmental departments where lawyers specialise in environmental legislation such as pollution control and waste management.

Environmental lawyers may also be employed by large companies or organisations to ensure compliance with regulations or to deal with issues of litigation.

Countryside and forestry management

Although most of the jobs in this area are within the public sector, there are some private landowners and companies that require staff to develop, manage or protect their land. There is a range of job titles including: countryside manages, officers or advisers, wildlife rangers, foresters, forest workers.

One major airport has even recruited an ecologist to save as much flora and fauna as possible during the construction of a runway. To date, he has helped save 16,000 newts, 3,000 frogs and 13,000 toads from bulldozers! (The *Times*, 26 May 1998.)

BEING A CONSULTANT

Consultants are usually employed in an advisory capacity on an 'ad hoc' rather than permanent basis. Not only do private sector companies employ consultants, but also the public and voluntary sectors often buy in their services.

In general a consultant's role is to advise the company on the impact of their activities on the environment. Sometimes companies call in con-

- Effects of environmental change (grazing, disturbance, climate and land use change).

- Mechanisms of plant adaptation to environmental stress.

- Development of a population modelling framework to support the management of a conservation area for bottlenose dolphins.

- Population dynamics and evolutionary genetics of insects.

- Microbial transformations of toxic metals, relevance to pollution.

- Impact of cyanobacterial and algal toxins and blooms on water quality.

- Development of wind, solar and wave energy.

- Exposure to chemical pollutants in the environment and the effects on human health.

Fig. 2. Examples of research and development topics.

sultants to 'trouble shoot' – diagnose problems and suggest solutions. The lucky ones procure long-term contracts to manage a specific project.

The consultant has to carry out a great deal of research before coming up with an action plan for the senior management of the organisation.

Specialising as a consultant

The environmental field is so wide that it is usual for consultants to specialise in one environmental aspect. For instance, there are environmental consultancies specialising in noise, water, environmental control, auditing or impact assessment. Other private consultancy firms – planning, surveying, architecture, design and engineering – take into account environmental aspects and issues in their work. Some consultants may specialise in working with one type of industry, such as construction or retail.

There may also be opportunities for experienced consultants in other countries, mainly on a short-contract basis.

It is most unusual to become a consultant straight from university, as companies expect you to have many years' related experience after graduating.

WORKING IN RESEARCH AND DEVELOPMENT

Research and development work generally means working for research institutes or multi-national companies. Scientific research is very expensive to carry out and research posts are often funded by various organisations and bodies, such as universities, central government, government agencies, Higher Education Funding Councils or private organisations. For this reason, many are not permanent posts but fixed term contracts for the duration of the funding (usually from one to three years).

All kinds of scientists, research assistants and technicians are recruited, depending on the industry and the type of research and development required. Relevant degree disciplines range from astrophysics and ecology through to hydrogeology and zoology.

Applied research

There are also opportunities for postgraduates to undertake applied research within organisations. Field work, together with data analysis and report writing, are key aspects of such posts. Staff may work within teams, often participating in all aspects of a number of research and development programmes, including project formulation, implementation and reporting.

ENTRY AND QUALIFICATIONS

In this growing area, with so many different jobs and employers, there is no one route in. However, the private sector is very similar to the public sector in terms of the qualifications required (see pages 31-34).

Environmental science as a first degree is not always regarded as particularly useful. This may be because there are a large number of them with different content and focus. Only some are science-based, others specialise in countryside management or geography. Many employers prefer applicants to have first degree qualifications in a traditional subject (for example, sciences, engineering, town planning) followed by specialist training or a postgraduate degree or diploma in the relevant environmental topic.

- Private sector employers may state age restrictions for posts and often target their recruitment at newly qualified graduates or post-graduates. As with the public sector, competition is tough for environmentally related posts, so the more qualifications and experience you have the better.

- Many posts involve multi-disciplinary teamwork, where it is vital to be able to liaise with other professionals in non-environmental disciplines. Communication and interpersonal skills are therefore very important.

- Some organisations offer postgraduates sponsored scholarships to study an environmentally related topic. Check out the publication *Sponsorships for Students*.

Experience and commitment
Previous voluntary experience shows commitment as well as allowing you to develop your skills, In order to demonstrate your knowledge and interest, aim to keep up-to-date and informed on the latest environmental issues. Read magazines, newsletters of environmental organisations (see Additional Resources) and the national and local press.

Specific job-related information

Environmental impact assessment, auditing, accounting and law
Many environmentally related degree courses cover these topics, such as:

- Environmental Management
- Environmental Control
- Environmental Risk management
- Environmental Planning
- Environmental Monitoring and Assessment.

These courses can only give an overview of the various topics. They are useful in that they give you a certain amount of knowledge of the issues involved in environmental legislation or impact assessment. However, doing a module or a semester on environmental law does not qualify you to practise as an environmental lawyer. For that, you need to qualify first as a lawyer and then specialise in environmental law.

Year 1
Environmental biology, environmental chemistry, environmental microbiology, environmental physics, environmental risk perception, European legal studies, foundation mathematics and statistics.

Year 2
Chemical monitoring, computer modelling and data analysis, electronic signal processing, environmental biomonitoring, environmental risk assessment, the working environment, health and safety management, research methods, optional work placements.

Year 3
Environmental auditing, environmental impact assessment, integrative studies, pollution management, eco-safety, project.

Fig. 3. Typical content of an Environmental Risk Management course.

Consultancy work
Some consultancies may recruit graduates to carry out research work before 'letting them loose' on clients. However, the majority recruit people with many years' experience post-degree, who have further qualifications and training to their name. The most successful consultants have expert knowledge and experience of their specialist industry or field as well as environmental qualifications.

Reseach and development
It is possible to enter research and development as a research assistant or research technician with a Higher National Certificate or Diploma or equivalent and some experience of laboratory work. However, degree level qualifications are often required.

CASE STUDIES

Advising others
With a degree in chemical engineering and a postgraduate qualification in pollution studies, Julia started her career as an environmental and safety coordinator in an oil company. Her role was to advise senior management on how to minimise the impact of company activities on the

environment. She had to be up-to-date on all the relevant environmental legislation and issues. She has now moved to another company within the energy sector to gain more experience. Her work involves liaising with government departments and environmental pressure groups such as Friends of the Earth, as well as other divisions within the company.

Designs on the future

Marcus works for a landscape design consultancy where he is currently involved in designing the grounds and surroundings of the headquarters of an international finance company. He has to take into account the clients' wishes as well as those of the wider community. 'The client concentrates on the importance of the image of the company – I consider that, of course, but also advise the client on the impact of the project on the environment.' Marcus chose landscape architecture as a career as he felt it combined his love of art, the landscape and gardening. As part of his degree (BA Hons in landscape architecture) he spent time with a small private landscape consultancy. This practical work experience helped enormously when he came to apply for jobs.

Planning changes to the environment

Ben went into town planning from a desire 'to see tangible changes to the environment as a direct result of my input'. As he knew what he wanted to do, he decided on a town planning degree rather than a more generalist one such as geography or economics. After graduating, he chose to work in the private sector as he feels it gives him more opportunity to work for a variety of different employers, from architects, planners and urban designers to research organisations and chartered surveyors. He started out on his career as an assistant with a planning consultancy, gaining promotion to project manager after two years. He then broadened his experience by moving to a large firm of chartered surveyors as a senior planner. After being promoted to an associate of the company, he was headhunted for his present position of head of planning for a rival firm of chartered surveyors. One day he hopes to set up his own planning consultancy business.

CHECKLIST

1. What could be the advantages and disadvantages of working in the private sector as opposed to the public sector?

2. What would motivate you to work in this area?

3. Why are jobs in this area on the increase now?

4. Where will you look for vacancies?

5. What are the different types of environmentally related jobs in industry and commerce?

6. If you are clear about which career to follow, what qualifications do you need?

7. Draw up a list of any first degree subjects in this field that interest you.

8. How can you demonstrate to an employer that you are interested and committed to environmentally related work?

9. How could you find out about student sponsorship deals?

4
Working for Voluntary and Statutory Organisations

FINDING OUT WHO THE EMPLOYERS ARE

The voluntary and statutory sectors play a vital role in conserving and improving the environment.

The large number of voluntary, independently funded and government funded bodies offer a variety of opportunities for working with the environment.

To list all such organisations would take up too much space in this book, so a few of the major ones only are mentioned. The directories of *Who's Who in the Environment* (The Environment Council) give a more comprehensive listing of organisations concerned with various aspects of the environment.

It is worth remembering that many voluntary organisations and charities do not have unlimited resources and so a large stamped self-addressed envelope enclosed with any enquiry would be welcome.

Job opportunities are varied, depending on the organisation, and include:

- practical 'hands-on' conservation work (countryside rangers/ officers, project managers, scientists, scientific officers)
- management
- fundraising
- press and information
- administration and clerical work.

Employment can take several forms, such as long-term or short-term volunteering, low paid, unpaid or paid work. There are more opportunities for voluntary work (unpaid or low paid) than there are for paid posts in these sectors.

48

CONSERVING, IMPROVING AND REGENERATING THE ENVIRONMENT

Below are some of the many organisations whose work is to protect, improve and care for the environment.

British Trust for Conservation Volunteers (BTCV)

This charitable organisation aims to involve people of all ages in practical conservation work in rural and urban areas. It has a large network of over 1,300 offices and 2,000 local groups dedicated to local voluntary action for the environment and works in partnership with a number of different organisations.

BTCV is a leading provider of practical conservation training. It runs over 200 courses a year throughout the UK, covering a wide range from hedgelaying, wildlife gardening and managing wetlands to health and safety and leadership. It also runs short working holidays (Natural Breaks) in this country as well as abroad (for people aged at least 16 years old). It is also worth noting that taking part in a Natural Break can qualify you for the residential project of the Duke of Edinburgh's Gold Award.

Every year BTCV involves 95,000 volunteers in projects. From one day projects to long-term volunteer officer placements (for a minimum of three months), there is a full range of opportunities for people to gain experience in all aspects of practical conservation, as well as the administrative and management responsibilities supporting the work. Job descriptions for volunteers vary but may include work with schools and youth groups, supporting local communities, organising training courses, promoting local events and fundraising.

The Countryside Commission

This is the government's statutory adviser on countryside matters in England. Its equivalent in Wales is the Countryside Council for Wales and in Scotland the Scottish Natural Heritage (see below).

Its aim is to make sure that the countryside is protected and that it can be used and enjoyed both now and in the future. All three bodies work in partnership with other organisations, such as local authorities, public agencies, voluntary bodies, farmers, landowners and private individuals. Like English Nature (see below), they provide grants and advice for conservation projects and designate areas for the protection of habitats and wildlife.

Out of the 250 staff who work for the Countryside Commission, over half are based in regional offices around the country and the rest at the headquarters in Cheltenham. There are opportunities for environmental specialists such as planners and landscape architects as well as for ecologists and technical, administrative and support staff. The Countryside Commission does not, however, take on volunteers.

English Nature

This is the statutory body which 'achieves, enables and promotes nature conservation in England'. Sister organisations are responsible for Scotland and Wales. The aim of English Nature is to improve the wildlife and natural features of England, through sustainable management practices. To do this, it not only takes action itself but also works in partnership with government, agencies and voluntary organisations. English Nature offers discretionary grants to other organisations to help in achieving its aims. Some of the projects it has been involved in recently include:

- restoring and expanding key endangered habitats such as lowland heathland
- setting up a hydrophone link to listen to dolphins
- conserving one of England's rarest and most threatened plants – the Tintern spurge.

A major part of its role is to recommend sites as candidates for the term Sites of Special Scientific Interest (SSSIs). SSSIs, most of which are privately owned or managed, are notified by English Nature because of their plants, animals or geological or physiographical features. SSSI notification ensures extra protection of the area – latest figures from English Nature reveal that 90 per cent of the 4,000 SSSIs across England are managed in a way that maintains or improves their conservation value.

In addition to the necessary administrative, technical and support staff, English Nature employs a variety of specialist staff, such as scientists, land agents, site managers and conservation officers. Conservation officers carry out visits to SSSIs, assessing the condition of the features of interest and recording information on current management and the causes of any decline in the condition of the site.

Unfortunately, English Nature cannot offer work placements at the current time due to reduced resources of staff, time and money.

Groundwork

Groundwork is an environmental regeneration organisation which helps people improve the environment and social and economic prospects of their local area. It works in partnership with the community, the local authority and local businesses in over 150 towns and cities. The organisation provides practical advice, information and support to individuals or community groups on environmental projects. On any one day the Groundwork organisation can be working on 4,000 projects. These projects can be anything from the reclamation of derelict and neglected land for a play area to the provision of environmental training for unemployed adults.

Businesses also benefit from the activities of Groundwork staff who offer advice and information on environmental management and issues. They also carry out environmental reviews ('green check ups') of a business's operations.

One of the many benefits of Groundwork to local schools and colleges is the 'hands on' help given in the delivery of environmental aspects of the curriculum. In 1998 the millionth child will have gone through its Education Programme.

Groundwork is involved in a series of Youth Programmes, which involve young people in practical educational projects to regenerate their neighbourhoods. For example, the Voluntary Projects Assistants programme is an initiative open to all unemployed graduates. Volunteers shadow a full-time member of Groundwork staff in a local project and also gain support in their job search. Groundwork say that nearly 80 per cent 'swiftly secure' paid employment after such experience.

According to Groundwork many staff start as volunteers in a local office. Recent job vacancies were for an environmental business coordinator (to coordinate the environmental improvement activity), a programme manager (to develop and manage diverse environmental programmes) and a community projects officer.

The National Trust

The National Trust is an independent charity involved in the conservation of open country and coastline areas, historic houses, industrial monuments, archaeological sites, gardens and wildlife areas. It is the country's largest single private landowner. Many of its sites are designated as nationally important by the statutory nature conservation bodies. The National Trust's aim is to preserve these places for the benefit of the nation. The equivalent in Scotland is the National Trust for Scotland.

The National Trust owns, either wholly or partially, over 400 SSSIs in England and Wales and 12 (called Areas of Special Scientific Interest) in Northern Ireland. It works in partnership with many other organisations involved in nature conservation.

Approximately 3,000 staff work for the National Trust in specialist roles such as countryside managers, land agents, archaeologists, foresters, architects and public relations officers or in technical, administrative, clerical and support roles.

There are a few traineeships (modern apprenticeships) known as Careerships offered in amenity horticulture or in countryside management (landscapes and ecosystems). These combine practical training with theoretical knowledge and understanding over three years, leading to NVQ levels 2 and 3. The Careerships are mainly for young people wanting to become gardeners or countryside wardens. Entry requirements are a minimum of four GCSEs (A-C) or equivalent including maths, English and science. There is stiff competition for these posts and applicants need to demonstrate clearly not only their academic ability but also their commitment to the Careership by their hobbies, work experience or volunteer work. It should also be noted that although training locations vary from year to year, it is likely that apprentices will have to live away from home.

Scottish Natural Heritage (SNH)

SNH is a non-departmental public body whose functions are 'to secure the conservation and enhancement of the natural heritage of Scotland' – its wildlife, habitats and landscapes. SNH was formerly the Nature Conservancy Council (the equivalent of English Nature) and the Countryside Commission for Scotland.

Many of SNH's staff are scientists trained in disciplines such as biology, botany or zoology. Graduates may also be recruited with other relevant degrees such as geography, ecology, geology, environmental studies, forestry, agriculture, science, planning or land management. Competition is fierce and vacancies are advertised in the national and/or local press and in appropriate specialist journals such as *New Scientist*.

The Wildlife Trusts

The Wildlife Trusts are a nationwide network of registered charity and voluntary organisations. The aim of the 46 local Trusts is to protect threatened wildlife and wildlife habitats in towns and in the countryside, so that others may enjoy them. They do this by managing nature reserves and campaigning on wildlife and countryside issues.

One of their most recent projects, working with the Environment Agency, has been to secure funding for an otter recovery programme. The otter was common in the UK in the 1950s but became almost extinct because of farm pollution and habitat loss (*The Times*, 8 June 1998).

The Trusts employ a variety of staff, including wardens, rangers, gamekeepers, managers, fundraisers, education officers and administrative staff. However, opportunities for employment are few. Joining your local trust as a volunteer will not only give you an insight into the work involved, but could also give you useful experience.

PUTTING ON THE PRESSURE

Opportunities also exist for anyone interested in active campaigning to change environmentally unfriendly policies and practices. There are a number of pressure or lobby groups such as Friends of the Earth, Greenpeace and the World Wide Fund for Nature.

One of the main criteria required for working in such organisations is a firm commitment to the protection and conservation of the environment.

Friends of the Earth (FOE)

Friends of the Earth is one of the UK's leading pressure groups to protect the environment. FOE England, Wales and Northern Ireland is part of the FOE International network which helps FOE national groups work together. It is now the largest international network of environmental groups in the world, covering more than 54 countries worldwide.

FOE England, Wales and Northern Ireland is made up of two separate organisations responsible for the overall running of FOE. FOE Limited is the campaigning and lobbying arm of FOE for environmental protection, conservation and the sustainable use of natural resources. Its mission is 'to campaign actively, effectively and imaginatively to protect and improve the conditions for life on earth, now and for the future.'

FOE Trust Limited is a registered charity, undertaking research, education and public information work on environmental and related social issues.

Just a few of FOE's successful campaigns include:

- forcing UK aerosol makers to stop using ozone-destroying CFCs
- stopping the hunting of otters in Britain
- persuading Parliament to pass five major environmental Acts
- stopping plans to build an unsafe nuclear waste dump.

FOE employs approximately 100 paid staff, mostly based in London. It takes on volunteers at its London office and regional offices and in over 240 voluntary local groups around the UK.

Greenpeace

Greenpeace is an international, independent environmental pressure group. It uses non-violent direct actions to campaign in the UK and internationally for industrial and political solutions to prevent abuse of the natural world. It is not only involved in environmental problem-solving and political lobbying, but also funds scientific research throughout the world and carries out educational work on environmental issues.

Greenpeace campaigns on many issues, for example to list but a very few:

● the threat to wildlife from the actions of humankind, pollution or natural disaster
● the disposal of toxic waste into rivers and seas
● the release of pollutants into the atmosphere
● genetically engineered food crops.

Greenpeace currently employs about 70 staff in its London office in various professional and support roles, such as personnel officers, public relations officers, lawyers, marketing directors, administrators, campaigners and scientists. Qualifications are required only where relevant to particular posts. However, relevant experience and knowledge are nearly always required.

Most of the voluntary help is needed with administration in the office. In fact, 95 per cent of the enquiries received in the Public and Supporter Information Unit are dealt with by a team of volunteers. Other volunteers help with the numerous Greenpeace local campaign groups throughout the country, assisting with fundraising, lobbying MPs, or participating in an action. Some volunteers are occasionally needed to assist in research, information technology, translation and other projects.

Greenpeace has offices around the world which offer various opportunities for volunteer participation. Applicants should write directly to individual offices. Greenpeace's Public Information Unit has a Greenpeace worldwide address list (see Useful Addresses for contact details).

World Wide Fund for Nature (WWF)

Formerly World Wildlife Fund, WWF is one of the largest conservation organisations in the world, operating in more than 100 countries. Its projects contribute to the conservation of natural habitats such as forests, grasslands, wetlands, coasts and marine areas. WWF is also involved in finding long-term practical solutions to the over-exploitation of natural resources such as wood, freshwater and fish.

One of its current campaigns evolved from the claim that Britain's woodlands are at risk. WWF hopes to convince all European governments to do more to protect such areas. Its staff surveyed forests in 15 countries checking on the levels of pollution, the amount of protected forest area, the standards of production and the national environmental, social and cultural policies applied to forests (*The Guardian*, 27 May 1998).

Opportunities for employment within WWF-UK may be limited, as it is primarily a fundraising organisation. Of the relatively small staff, most are in office-based posts with only a few directly involved with conservation work. When vacancies do arise, they are advertised in the national press and on the WWF-UK website. Entry is very competitive. However, volunteers are always welcome to help with local fundraising activities or to assist on conservation days.

There may also be job opportunities with WWF International, working abroad.

STARTING POINTS

Work experience

From the organisations mentioned above, it can be seen that there are few full-time paid jobs on offer. However, the voluntary or statutory sectors do offer the opportunity to gain valuable work experience, as most of them have a tradition of taking on volunteers. Indeed, many environmentalists started their careers as unpaid or low paid volunteers.

Depending on the job, some organisations will pay expenses or a small allowance to volunteers.

Training is usually on the job for volunteer workers. Paid volunteer organisers sometimes recruit, train and supervise volunteers, which can be useful for other management posts. Many organisations recruiting managers require candidates to have a track record in facilitating environmental projects and supervising volunteers.

Volunteers are often asked to make a regular commitment, for example of a day or more a week for at least three months. This is usually so that organisations can plan and allocate their resources accordingly.

It is important that applicants for volunteer posts give as much information about themselves as possible on the application form (see Figure 4). Volunteers are placed according to their skills and experience as well as their availability.

received: _____

For office use:	
Acknowledged	Registered

VOLUNTEER INFORMATION FORM
(please complete both sides)

Name ....
Supporter No. (if known and applicable)

Address

....

Postcode ....Telephone No. ....

Days Available		Time Available	
Days	Available	At what times during the day are you available?	
Monday	Yes/No		
Tuesday	Yes/No	During what dates are you available?	
Wednesday	Yes/No		
Thursday	Yes/No	How many days each week are you available?	
Friday	Yes/No		

How prepared are you to perform routine administrative tasks?

....

How able are you to guarantee a regular, long-term commitment?
(minimum 3 months)

....

To what extent do you enjoy working as part of a team?

....

How much do you feel able to work on your own initiative?

....

Do you have a good working knowledge of the English language?

....

Are you prepared to respect confidentiality?

....

What has been your interest in environmental issues to date?

....

Fig. 4. Example of a volunteer application form.

Please indicate in the boxes below the skills that you possess			
Skill	Please tick	Skill	Please tick
Keyboard (20-40 wpm)		Data Entry	
Keyboard (40+ wpm)		Full UK Driving Licence	If yes, are you over 23 years of age?
Computer Literacy		Office Administration	
Languages	Please specify:	Other skills	Please specify:
Switchboard Operation			
Qualified Librarian			
Library Research			

Please note below any other specialist skills you have, no matter how obscure or seemingly irrelevant:

Please note below any previous work experience, including voluntary work:

Emergency contact
- in case of accident, please give the name and daytime phone number of a person who you would wish us to contact

Name: Tel no:

Signature & date:

REFERENCES

Before we can take you on as a volunteer, we would like to take a reference. Please give the name, address and daytime telephone number of a person (not a friend or relative) from whom we can seek an opinion of your suitability for voluntary work

NAME ....

ADDRESS ....

....

TELEPHONE NUMBER..

Fig. 4. Cont/d

Paid work

The point which you enter employment will depend on your academic and/or vocational qualifications and/or your breadth of experience and skills. Qualifications and/or experience also determine whether you become involved in the decision-making and policy side of an organisation or the more practical skilled or unskilled hands-on side. For instance, someone with:

● *no academic qualifications* (but maybe with some experience) could become a gardener, forest worker, estate worker or even wildlife ranger. It should, however, be noted that an increasing number of applicants for wildlife ranger posts do hold qualifications.

● *some GCSEs or A levels or equivalent* could enter at technician level, doing administrative and practical jobs such as forestry, farming, gardening, countryside management, meteorology. Useful subjects would be sciences rather than arts – physics, chemistry, biology, maths or maths with statistics, geography, geology and economics. Four GCSEs (A-C) or equivalent including maths, science and English are required for entry to the National Trust's Careership scheme.

● *a first degree or postgraduate degree or diploma* could enter at the decision-making level, as a consultant, research scientist, manager or specialist in a particular environmental aspect.

In some organisations, however, experience and skills are more important than qualifications. Progression to other posts can be achieved by training and experience on the job, as well as through in-service training courses, college courses or outside training organisations.

CASE STUDIES

From temporary to permanent

Claire joined English Nature as a full-time conservation officer after working for them on a temporary contract for a couple of years. 'I had spent a year doing voluntary work with a Wildlife Trust and I think this experience helped considerably in me getting my foot in the door with English Nature, even though initially it was on a short-term contract.' She chose to do an environmental geography option in the third year of her geography degree which stimulated her interest in environmental work. She is based in the south-west of the country, working on various projects with the aim of protecting habitats or species, especially those on SSSIs. Her work as a conservation officer also involves advising landowners on environmental issues, and developing long-term plans for marine and coastal conservation.

A change of focus

Sophie left school after GCSEs and did not know what she really wanted to do. After four years in a clerical job with an insurance company, she decided to pursue her love of the outdoors. She had been on a few working holidays with BTCV and enjoyed it so much that she gave up her job and applied for a post as a volunteer officer for six months. She has now been accepted on to an HND course in environmental management.

Doing practical project work

After completion of his biology degree, Ahmed looked into a number of environmentally related careers. He was surprised at how difficult it was to enter such jobs, even though his qualifications were good. 'Employers were going for people with experience as well as qualifications.' He decided to postpone his job search and opted for a part-time postgraduate diploma course in conservation management. The part-time nature of the course meant he could spend some time gaining work experience on a farm. With experience and a relevant postgraduate qualification, he was able to get a part-time job with Groundwork, where he is now involved in environmental improvement projects. His work includes motivating volunteers and giving practical advice and help. He hopes to move into a full-time post eventually.

CHECKLIST

1. If you are considering voluntary work, are you looking for a challenge where you will gain as much as you give?

2. Voluntary work is generally unpaid or low paid – could you live on a modest income?

3. Voluntary work requires dedication and sometimes long working hours – have you got the stamina?

4. Research what volunteer opportunities exist in your area.

5. Where would you find a list of environmental organisations?

6. Which type of organisation interests you and why?

7. How firm is your commitment to protecting and conserving the environment?

7. Is there a particular aspect of work which attracts you in these sectors?

5
Finding Out What is Suitable for You

WHO ARE YOU?

Before choosing a job or career, it is important not only to think about what the work may be like, but also what you are like:

- What are you good at?
- What are you not so good at?
- What interests you?
- What kind of a person are you?

Once you have answered (honestly!) certain questions about yourself, you will find it easier to find out what type of work suits you. It is obviously good to aim for a career that best fits your skills and abilities.

TAKING STOCK

Taking stock of exactly who you are – your attributes, skills and interests – also enables you to discover if there are areas that need to be developed or improved. A bonus to doing a self-assessment exercise now is that, having identified all your skills and attributes, you can point them out to potential employers or course providers – either on your **curriculum vitae**, application form or in interviews. This may enhance your prospects of employment.

Listing your skills

Many people would find it difficult to list their skills if asked. It is sometimes easier to think of activities that you do and then consider the skills required to carry them out. So take a moment to look at all the areas of your life:

- home
- spare time activities
- school, college or university
- any work experience.

COLUMN 1

COLUMN 2

Home
Activities (list)

Skills involved

Spare time activities
Hobbies or interests (list)

School, college or university
Achievements (list)

Clubs or societies (list)

Work experience
Specific tasks

Fig. 5. Worksheet – activities.

What do you do in each of these areas? Look at each one and note down your various activities, how you behave and how you interact with other people. Use column 1 of the worksheet in Figure 5 on page 62 to help you.

Looking at each area

For example, under 'home', consider in what ways you help out in the family. Are you the one who plans the outings or comes up with imaginative ideas for celebrating birthdays? Do you spend any time looking after younger brothers or sisters? What role do you play in your home life?

Under 'spare time activities', list any hobbies or interests you have, for example sport, playing a musical instrument, socialising with friends, reading, dancing, drama, gardening, watching television, cooking.

Under 'school, college or university', list your achievements so far (however small) and what clubs or societies you have joined, if any.

Under 'work experience', think of actual experiences, whether it is babysitting, paper round, or working part-time in a shop, office or elsewhere. Then write down any specific tasks you carry out in the job.

Now you have filled in column 1 of the worksheet, you are beginning to gather information which will help you identify the type of person you are.

Identifying your skills

Column 2 of the worksheet takes you one stage further, noting the skills you already have. It should be easy to list the skills you display in all the different areas of your life. The trick is to remember a time when you were doing a particular activity and imagine you are doing it now. What exactly are you doing? What skills are you using to do what you do? What is your motivation for doing it?

Analysing yourself

For instance, if one of your interests is playing the piano, think about the self-discipline you need to practise, your sense of rhythm, the good hand/eye coordination you need to read and play the notes, your tolerance for repetitive work as you go up and down the scales one more time. Even watching television has skills attached to it – do you take time to select carefully what you watch? Do you discipline yourself to watch only so many hours? Do you use television to relax? Can you operate the video machine? Are you beginning to get the picture?

As a separate exercise, consider the implications of some of the

Tick which points apply to you

– I am hardworking ☐

– I am polite ☐

– I am usually on time for lessons/lectures ☐

– I get my work in on time ☐

– I get my work in before the deadline ☐

– I set myself goals ☐

– I plan how to use my time ☐

– My work is usually accurate ☐

– I am usually neat and tidy ☐

– I often take the lead in class ☐

– I take responsibility for my mistakes ☐

– I make friends relatively easily ☐

– I am a good listener ☐

– I am patient ☐

– I . . . ☐

Fig. 6. Worksheet – my good points.

activities you have listed. If your interests are solitary, does this mean you prefer to work on your own rather than with a team of people? If your activities are all very practical or involve being creative, is this what you are looking for in a career?

Personal characteristics

Now look at the worksheet on page 64 in Figure 6 and tick all the points that apply to you. Be honest. Add to the bottom of the list any other good points you have.

For instance, you may wish to include adaptability, confidence, initiative, persuasiveness, sensitivity or tact. What others can you think of? Again, consider the different areas of your life. Are you unselfish – do you take other people's views into account before your own? Are you a good listener – do others confide in you?

It is important at this stage to ask someone who knows you well, a friend or a member of your family, for their opinion. Show them the list of good points and ask them to tick the ones that they think apply to you. You might find you have been too modest and you have more good points than you thought!

Finding examples

Now comes the interesting part – thinking of situations where you demonstrate each good point you have ticked. Ask your friend for examples too. By doing this exercise, you are coming up with concrete examples to justify your claims. Employers often ask for such evidence.

GETTING IT RIGHT

You should by now have a clear idea of where your skills lie and what type of person you are. It is now important to find out what employers are looking for and if you match the skills and personality they want.

Employer requirements

Change in organisations is now taken as the norm rather than the exception, and they therefore need to be able to respond flexibly to the different challenges and opportunities presented. They need their staff to be flexible too, to be able to use them in whatever way is necessary, often at short notice. Employers want people who can switch easily from task to task, or handle more than one task at a time. For this reason, they look for a broad range of skills and a rounded personality in their staff. Candidates with some non-academic activities are welcomed, as it shows they have some balance in their lives. As seen above, such activities can also show evidence of various skills.

Core skills
The **core skills**, such as those learnt while studying for your GCSEs, are common requirements by employers:

● Communicating – good reading, writing, speaking and listening skills.

● Using numbers – accurate and confident with money, measurements, graphs, diagrams, statistics.

● Using computers – confident with word processing and spreadsheets.

● Working with people – teamwork, taking responsibility, leading, following instructions.

● Working alone – understanding where and when you need help, setting goals.

● Problem solving – finding the right answers and ignoring the wrong ones.

Employers want people who can get on well with others, express themselves clearly (by, for example, explaining, putting over a point of view), understand instructions and work well in a team.

Transferable skills
There is an increasing emphasis these days on work-related **transferable skills**. These are skills that are not specific to any one job but are general to many. They can therefore be transferred between occupations and areas of work, such as:

● The ability to plan and organise.
● Teamwork – working and cooperating with others.
● Interpersonal skills.
● Decision-making skills.
● The ability to concentrate on more than one task at once.
● The ability to prioritise.
● The ability to work to deadlines.

Transferable skills are important in a labour market where frequent job changes are not unusual. You will develop some of the skills during your time in education, some while at home and others while in the workplace. How many more transferable skills can you think of? Consider again the activities you carry out from day to day. Can you add time management to your list? Do you manage your time effectively by planning your work, getting your assignments or projects done on time?

Once you are in employment, think about the skills you have which can be transferred to other jobs. For example:

● A secretary can be skilled at understanding instructions and paying attention to detail, which are useful skills for any other job.

● Scientists use logical thinking, observation, deduction, imagination and curiosity in their job – all qualities that can be useful in many other occupations.

It is worth noting down the skills you have that are relevant to more than one job, so that you can convince employers that you will be an effective member of their workforce. It also means that they will not have to spend time training you in such skills.

Making up any shortfalls

Some jobs call for specialist skills, such as artistic, linguistic, technical, scientific or other specific job-related skills. It is important when choosing which career direction to go in that you consider which specific skills will be required. Can you develop and improve the skills you already have or do you need to acquire new ones?

When looking at career areas, always have the following three questions in mind:

● Which skills are required for this particular job?
● Which skills do you have already?
● Which skills do you need to develop?

During your working life, this should be an exercise you do on a regular basis, particularly when considering a career change. If there are skills you need but do not yet have, then you can investigate the ways and means of developing or acquiring them.

It may be helpful to rate your skill level on a scale of 1-5 as follows:

5 – I am extremely good at this (no further development required).

4 – I am good at this (but I could do better).

3 – I am OK at this (I can get by but may need to develop this skill further if I want to progress in my job or move on to other jobs).

2 – I am not too good at this (do I need to develop and improve this skill?).

1 – I have not got a clue about this (do I need this skill?).

This may help give you an indication of which direction you want to go in and how you can develop in your career.

Learning for life

It is important to remember that any work experience and skills previously acquired will never be wasted, as they may be transferable to a new career.

You can lower your risk of unemployment by building on your existing skills, learning new ones and being aware of opportunities for career development. If you do not do so, your skills may become redundant. It is important to adapt to changing circumstances and be willing to continue to learn.

Lifelong learning is seen as the key to getting and keeping work and developing a satisfying career in the future.

LEARNING RESOURCES

It is important when finding out what career direction is suitable for you to use all the resources around you. Some of the resources available to you may include:

- Careers library – school, college and university careers resources contain various books, leaflets, videos and often computer programs which can help by giving you concrete information about the different career areas.

- Case studies, such as the ones in this book – these can give you an idea of what routes other people have taken and whether any would suit you.

- Friends and family – important resources. They know you almost as well as, if not better than, you know yourself. They can certainly give you a different perspective on any ideas you may have.

- People doing the job – it is vital to be able to get the opinions of people actually doing a job you are interested in. It may be that you already know someone or know of someone and can ask them for information (see below 'Getting specific information' for guidelines on what to ask). If not, see if your careers adviser can put you in touch with someone. You can also read the many career books, magazines, leaflets and videos with profiles of real people doing jobs that interest you. Again, ask your careers adviser or teacher for advice.

- Professional bodies – these often have information packs about their profession. Choose which ones to contact from the address list at the back of this book.

- Employers – these are an important source of information. The personnel department often has information packs not only about the organisation but often about the career area as well.

- Teachers – they may have an indication of your likelihood of getting the grades or exams necessary for certain careers. It may be worthwhile talking to them about your chances.

- Careers advisers – these are an invaluable source of information. They have information on all the different careers, training courses, college and university courses. They also have information on employers. Find out who your careers adviser is and use him or her.

- Work experience – this can be useful in many ways. If you have work experience in an area which interests you, it can give you a lot of specific information about the various jobs and whether you still want to pursue this idea. If it is not an area which interests you, you can still find out information about yourself and how you prefer to work – in a team or on your own, using your initiative or waiting for instructions, etc.

- The Internet – a wonderful source of information. Check out the websites of environmentally related organisations (see Additional Resources) and any other related websites.

Getting specific information

The more you structure your research, the better will be the information you gather. It is also easier to carry out research if you have some idea

of what you want to find out. Start by considering exactly what you need
to know that will help you decide to pursue your career idea. For
instance, is it the qualifications required, the training offered, the salary,
prospects of advancement or what the job involves on a day-to-day
basis? Only you will know.

Asking questions
If you get the opportunity to ask someone about the job they do, be specific in your questioning. Most people like talking about their work, so
it helps to have definite questions in mind, or you could end up spend-
ing half an hour listening to something you are not interested in or which
does not help you in your decision-making!
Specific questions could cover:

1. What made them choose their job?
2. What do they like about it?
3. What is not so good about it?
4. How many hours a day do they have to work?
5. What training did they have to do? (Be careful here as qualifications
    and training change and what they had to do might differ consider-
    ably from what you may have to do, but it may still give you some
    idea of what is involved.)
6. What sort of person do you need to be to do their work?
7. What skills do you need?

Depending on what information you have already, you may have a
whole list of other questions to ask. It may help to record the answers in
some way to review them later, for instance on a tape recorder or in a
notebook (see 'Career direction record' below).

DECIDING WHICH DIRECTION TO GO IN

So how do you decide which career to follow? There are many decisions
which only you can make, such as which area interests you, for example
architecture or science, conservation or environmental health, engineering or ecology? The information you have gathered by following the
advice in the previous pages will help you here.
It is also important to consider how involved you want to be in
protecting, improving or conserving the environment. There are options
to work behind the scenes in a support role, for instance in administration, personnel or education. Alternatively you might wish to be more
actively involved in a project management or hands-on role. The self-

assessment exercises you have done will give you vital information about you as a person and what you like or dislike.

Some decisions will be made for you. For instance, the level at which you enter a career depends on your qualifications and experience in the first instance. What you have to decide is what level you aspire to and therefore what qualifications and experience you need. It is then up to you to get these (see Chapter 7 for further help and information about becoming skilled and qualified).

Keeping options open

It is helpful to think in terms of a broad range of possible areas of work as a first step. Keep your options open for as long as you can by choosing a balance of subjects. Recognise that your career ideas may change, and remain as flexible and open to new ideas as possible. The core and transferable skills mentioned above help in moving between occupations and areas of work.

MOVING FORWARD

It is very useful to go over the exercises in this chapter, reviewing and reflecting on any decisions or opinions. This often gives a sense of achievement and the satisfaction of knowing exactly where you are now. You can then develop more easily a clear action plan and motivation for your future career planning.

You should now have a clear idea of what information you need to help make any first career decisions. If you do not, go back over the Learning Resources section and note what help you might need and who can give it to you.

Career direction record

It is very useful to keep some record of the information you gather about yourself and any career ideas you have. For example, if you interviewed anyone about their career, making a note of your thoughts afterwards can help clarify your ideas. Having easy access to a list of your skills and attributes saves time and effort when filling in application forms or going for interviews. Noting down why certain career areas hold your attention also helps when employers or course admissions tutors ask what prompted your interest.

Action plan

If you do not have an action plan, you may find that time flies by so quickly that you miss opportunities because you were not prepared.

Depending on what stage you are at in your career decision-making, it can be useful to list the activities you need to do now which will help you move forward. By looking at the resources available to you and the information you still need, this should be an easy task. It is vital to be specific, for instance:

● You may decide you need to join certain clubs or societies to expand your interest or make useful contacts. Which ones specifically? How will you find out? By when?

● You may want some work experience – who will you contact and when?

● Exactly what information do you still need? How are you going to get it?

It is important to remember that any career planning needs to be constantly reviewed as people change as time passes and often so do their ideas, hopes and dreams.

CASE STUDY

Gaining confidence

Judy is finishing her A-levels and GNVQ Advanced qualifications and hoping to go into a job. She carried out a self-assessment exercise and made the following comment: 'When I was asked what skills I had, you could have put them on the back of a postage stamp. Yet now in my file I have almost two pages of skills! Doing this exercise has given me more confidence in myself which I am sure will help when I go for jobs.'

CHECKLIST

1. Make sure you carry out the self-assessment quiz and can identify your skills.

2. What skills do you need now? What might you need in the future?

3. List the skills employers are generally looking for.

4. Skills can be transferred from one job to another. Which of your skills are transferable?

5. Improve your job applications by emphasising the qualities and skills you already have.

6. What have you learnt about your interests and the sort of job area which might interest you?

7. How can you find out about the actual work people do?

8. What resources are available to you?

9. Think in terms of a broad range of possible areas of work as a first step.

10. Start your action planning now.

6
Moving Towards Employability

SHOWING COMMITMENT

One way of ensuring that employers take your application seriously is to show them your commitment to their organisation and to an environmentally related career. This applies whether you want to work directly or indirectly for the environment, ie in a hands-on or support role. Evidence looked for includes the following:

- Membership of relevant clubs or societies, such as natural history, gardening, science or conservation.

- Membership of environmental organisations, such as the National Trust, Greenpeace, British Trust for Conservation Volunteers, World Wide Fund for Nature, Friends of the Earth. See Useful Addresses for contact details.

- Subscription to relevant magazines or journals, showing that you are up-to-date with current issues. See Additional Resources for examples.

- An awareness of the current global environmental concerns. As well as magazines and journals, there are also newspapers and the Internet which are all good sources of information.

- Relevant experience (see below).

- Knowledge of the organisation and the job. Ask for information from the personnel department and also see if there is any news about the organisation or the career area in the local or national press. Contact the relevant professional body (see Useful Addresses). Is there anyone you know who is doing a similar job, or anyone you know in the organisation who can give you information? Find out as much as possible.

● Working holidays, for instance with organisations such as the British Trust for Conservation Volunteers (Natural Breaks) and the National Trust (Working Holidays, short residential camps).

UNDERSTANDING THE IMPORTANCE OF EXPERIENCE

The first step of breaking into employment is often the hardest. You need experience to get a job and you need a job to get experience. In addition, since competition for available jobs is fierce, experience counts for a lot.

You can gain experience through work experience while at school, college or university, either during term-time or during vacations. You can also gain relevant experience before or while searching for a job or during periods of unemployment. A note of caution, however – check to make sure that this does not affect any unemployment benefit you may be claiming.

Experience can be in the form of practical, hands-on work or observation of someone's role (work shadowing). It may be voluntary, low paid or unpaid work. It is likely that you can negotiate for at least your expenses to be paid and in some cases you may even receive an allowance or a wage.

> **Whatever your experience, work experience will certainly be an introduction into the world of work – an *experience* of work – and one that employers value.**

What's in it for you?

Any type of work placement gives you the chance to develop all kinds of skills and strengths, such as communication, teamwork and self-confidence.

A learning experience

What you are offered may not be exactly what you wanted or had in mind. However, the key is to remember that any experience, whether good, bad or unexpected, is a learning experience and one you can benefit from. Ask yourself afterwards: what did you like or dislike about it? What does that tell you about yourself? In fact, employers might be even more impressed if you explain that although the experience was not your first choice, you benefited from it in many ways. This shows a level of maturity. For instance, did any of the following apply to you:

- gaining in confidence
- working in a team
- finding out what it is like to do different jobs
- having the experience of doing a full day's work
- meeting new people
- finding out what people do
- seeing different jobs being done
- finding out what you are good at – and not so good at.

There may be many other things you learnt while on a work experience. You may even gain some qualifications – volunteers with BTCV (see Chapter 4) can work towards vocational qualifications. Remember to write down anything significant in your career direction record for future reference.

Relevant work experience
This allows you to see whether you enjoy the work (it tests your interest), to learn new skills and to demonstrate your commitment to the environment to future employers. It may also give you the chance to build up a network of important contacts, new friends and people who share your concern for the environment. It is possible you could learn more about environmental issues and gain an insight into the work of large and small organisations. In addition, if you are seen to do a good job, it might open the door to a more permanent paid position. You will certainly be able to find out about any internal vacancies. You can gain all this and do some good for the environment too!

Make the most of it
Capitalise on your experience, whatever it is, by referring to it in your curriculum vitae and application forms. Ask for references (before you leave) from your work experience or placement employers.

ACQUIRING EXPERIENCE

How to obtain it
While you are in education, it may be that work experience is organised for you. However, there may come a time when you have to organise it yourself or when you decide you need some specific understanding of a career area or post. You can get this in a variety of ways, for example through low paid work, paid work, voluntary work, work shadowing or through the pursuit of hobbies or interests. Your circumstances and preferences will decide which you aim for.

Paid work

As already stated, many employers will be interested in your past experience before taking you on in a permanent position. However, it may still be possible, depending on your skills, qualifications and personality, to obtain some paid work without any particular experience. Some work may be available on a part-time, short-term or contract basis.

Contact organisations whose work interests you. It is often best to respond to specific vacancies, but speculative letters have been known to work on occasion (remember to enclose a stamped self-addressed envelope). Find out as much as you can beforehand about vacancies and application procedures. Also ask your school, college or university careers adviser if they can help you. Remember to use the Internet, if you have access to it, for vacancy information.

Volunteering

Many environmental organisations welcome volunteers. See below for a list and also look in the local and national press for vacancies, for instance, *The Guardian*'s volunteers pages on a Wednesday. Even if some organisations do not state that they take volunteers, it may be worth asking if you can simply work for free or work-shadow someone for a short period of time.

Be prepared to be interviewed. Not only do employers want to know who they are letting in to their organisation, but you may also find yourself up against competition – even volunteer jobs are limited.

For how long do you want to work?

For voluntary work, you will almost certainly be asked for some indication of the hours you are prepared to work. Although some organisations request volunteers to make a regular commitment of time for a set period, others may be more flexible and open to negotiation. The important thing is not to commit yourself to something you are unable to deliver, but to be honest and realistic at the time of application.

Opportunities may be short-term or long-term, depending on the organisation and the job. Some posts may be for specific times of year only. For example, the Royal Society for the Protection of Birds requires volunteer wardens mainly for the summer months only. It is up to you to decide what time you have available and when.

Needing more information?

If you are interested in volunteering, consider contacting not only the organisations listed in Figure 7, but also the National Centre for Volunteering (see Useful Addresses) for more information and details of

---

VOLUNTEERS WELCOME
Some of the organisations which welcome volunteers
for work in the UK

- British Trust for Conservation Volunteers – practical conservation work.
- Friends of the Earth – a variety of administrative work for the protection of the environment.
- The National Trust – conservation and restoration work.
- Nature Conservation Trusts – conservation work.
- The Prince's Trust – Volunteers – practical environmental projects within the community.
- Royal Society for the Protection of Birds – volunteer wardens.
- The Wildfowl and Wetlands Trust – administrative.
- The Wildlife Trusts – protection of threatened wildlife (administrative or practical outdoor work).
- World Wide Fund for Nature – local fundraising activities.

Fig. 7. List of organisations welcoming volunteers.

opportunities. Another source of information is the Youth for Britain database of volunteer opportunities both in the UK and abroad for students aged between 16 and 25. This is available in many careers service companies, schools and colleges as part of the ECCTIS 2000 UK Course Discover database.

Working holidays

Working holidays are also a good source of gaining experience. For example, you may get a taste of practical conservation activities, such as dry stone walling, step building, hedgelaying, pond digging and so on. Not only will this give you valuable experience, but it will also give you a sense of achievement, not least from the fact that you are making a positive contribution to the environment in some way. Remember that working holidays are usually not free – you may have to pay something towards your keep.

Pursuing your interests

By being a member of a club or society in your spare time, it may be that you are gaining useful experience in all kinds of ways. For instance, the following are just a few of the things you may have the opportunity to gain experience in:

- chairing meetings
- organising events
- being a committee member
- working with others
- contributing ideas
- dealing with finance (as treasurer)
- working on projects
- fundraising.

Some people, through an interest they have in the environment, also give up some of their time to contribute to the activities of an organisation. There is an example of one such person in the case study on page 82. In this way, the experience they gain is a bonus, while at the same time they are enjoying themselves or doing something they would do anyway.

GETTING A FOOT IN THE DOOR

Work experience

Any form of work experience offers the opportunity of getting a foot in the door with prospective employers. It gives you the chance to get your face known, make useful contacts and learn of any vacancies that might be coming up. By keeping your ear to the ground and meeting with other people, you are well placed to find out about vacancies either within the organisation in which you are working or within other organisations. Ensure colleagues and bosses know you are looking for a more permanent, paid, position. Do your best to increase your chances of employability and make the most of your work experience by:

- making yourself as useful as possible
- understanding as much as you can about the work you do
- learning about the work of others
- appreciating the overall aims and objectives of the organisation.

Even if you are not offered a permanent post, at least you will not have wasted a good learning opportunity, which will be of value to other employers. The good impression you created can also be mentioned in a reference which you can take to other employers.

Using your contacts

Using your contacts, or networking as it is often known, is another very good way of increasing your chances of employment. By networking, you are:

- giving yourself the chance to obtain information which may eventually lead to a job opportunity

- gaining informal access to the hidden job market – to jobs that may not even exist or have not yet been advertised

- meeting people you know or do not know, talking to them and gaining information and new contacts.

Creating your network

Start by deciding who your contacts are. Make a list of anyone you meet – anyone at all – as you go about your daily work and play. They may be people you know well such as friends, family and neighbours or people you know less well like colleagues, teachers, lecturers, friends of friends, acquaintances and so on. Now decide how each of them can help you (and if possible, how you can help them).

To widen the network even further, ask your friends, family, colleagues, friends of friends and acquaintances for the names of people they know who could help you and add them to your list.

Making contact

The next stage is to choose who you are going to approach first and so set up a meeting (either informally or formally, depending on who it is). It is important that you are clear at the beginning about what you want from the meeting. Remember that you may only have a short time to get your message across. Draw up a list of questions you can ask. They might include some of the following:

- Suggestions about career direction.
- Information about a particular organisation – people, aims, objectives, types of work, current projects.
- Developments within the career area or organisation.
- Ideas or suggestions about skills or attributes you may need to work on.
- Comments on your CV if relevant or appropriate.
- Names of anyone else who could help you.

Remember to add any new names to your ever-growing list of

contacts. Always thank your contact for their time and help, either by a follow-up telephone call or a letter. Consider too how you might help the person in return, either now or in the future.

Being proactive, not reactive

Some people may prefer a more passive role, waiting for the right vacancy to be advertised. They may see networking as difficult to do, either feeling shy or believing that they are imposing on people. However, people who actively use networking in their jobsearch find that most people enjoy helping others, provided the approach is right. Asking someone for a job is probably not the right approach! Asking for their advice or some specific information could be.

Worthwhile – and fun

Remember that any contact is a useful source of information and advice and may get you a step nearer to employment. Even if your networking does not lead directly or immediately to a job, at least you open yourself up to having an interesting and fun time in the process by meeting and talking with people! You will almost certainly learn something new from the experience too.

WHAT EMPLOYERS ARE LOOKING FOR

In addition to appropriate qualifications and knowledge, there are certain core skills and attributes which employers look for, no matter what position (paid or unpaid) you are applying for:

- an interest in, and commitment to, the aims of the particular organisation
- an ability to work with others
- a willingness to perform routine tasks
- a flexible approach to work
- an ability to work on your own initiative.

By ensuring you can give evidence of all the above, you will inevitably make yourself more employable and give yourself a better chance of succeeding in the jobs market.

QUESTIONS AND ANSWERS

Are employers really interested in any experience, even if it is not particularly relevant to the job being advertised?

Yes, because it can demonstrate to them any number of your skills as well as your attitude to work in general. It also gives them a referee to contact, to find out what kind of employee you were. However, if the experience is of direct relevance to the job in question, it will obviously give you more of a competitive edge.

What if I cannot make a regular commitment of time to a voluntary organisation?
You may be able to offer your services for a set period of time instead. It is always worth talking to people, explaining what you can and cannot do and seeing if you can come to some kind of mutual agreement.

Why shouldn't I ask contacts for a job?
In the first place, it is unlikely that there will be many on your list who will be able to oblige you with a job. Secondly, if they cannot give you a job, they will probably be thinking how to let you down gently, instead of thinking creatively how to help you. So it is better to ask them something it is in their power to give you – their advice or information. In this way, you are more likely to impress them should they ever be in a position to offer you work or influence the people who can.

CASE STUDIES

Pursuing an interest
Nick is an information technology specialist in a local authority. He is totally committed to conservation and uses his weekends, holidays and any other spare time he has to work for a nature conservation organisation. He can often be seen on his local beach either counting terns as part of a bird census or identifying different flora and fauna. He would love to do this as a full-time job but does not think he can afford to take a drop in salary at the moment. He is hoping that when he does make a decision to have a complete career change, the experience he is getting in his spare time will stand him in good stead. In the meantime he is just enjoying helping in an area he feels passionate about.

Making the most of an opportunity
When Josh was offered the chance to work-shadow a recycling officer, he was hoping to get out and about, visiting recycling sites around the county and seeing other council departments. However, the week he was due to work-shadow coincided with a major recycling publicity campaign and the recycling officer was called upon to help with the administrative work. After shadowing for a while, Josh asked if there was anything practical he could do to help. He was asked to distribute incoming

mail around the department and carry out some photocopying. This meant he was able to meet people in different jobs, gaining more insight into the varied work of the environment services department than he would otherwise have had.

Plugging the gap

After leaving university with a degree in ecology, Petra was finding it hard to find work. She could not get past stage one of the recruitment and selection process. 'Application forms ask for details of any work experience, which is of course practically nil, as I went to university straight from school. So no experience, no interview.' In her vacations, Petra chose to travel rather than work, so could not list summer work experience either.

Her university careers adviser suggested doing some voluntary work as an answer. Petra decided to commit herself to three days a week volunteering for a minimum of three months, which would leave two days a week for job search. In a relatively short time, she found an opening with her local wildlife trust. Now able to put down on application forms that she was working as a volunteer, she discovered her employability increasing almost immediately as she began to be shortlisted for interviews. She also found that employers were impressed by her commitment to a three-month volunteer period.

CHECKLIST

1. How can you show your commitment to an employer?

2. How could you keep yourself up to date with knowledge of developments in your field?

3. Do you belong to any relevant clubs, societies or organisations?

4. How would work experience benefit you?

5. Consider the different ways of gaining experience – which would suit you?

6. Is there any local organisation which takes on volunteers?

7. Volunteering demands a level of commitment – can you offer this?

8. If you have no other spare time, would you be prepared to have a working holiday?

9. Make a list of all the people you know and start networking.

7
Becoming Skilled and Qualified

Competition for environmentally related jobs is intense and is often from highly qualified people. Many graduates enter non-graduate jobs when they first leave university. Therefore, the more qualifications and experience you have, the more chances you are giving yourself to get to the interview stage of job recruitment and selection. Becoming skilled and qualified should however not be something that is 'done' to you, but a process of learning that involves you in an active role.

> **The more responsibility you take for your own learning and career development the more in control of your career path you will be.**

HOW WE LEARN

We are all unique individuals with our own way of doing things. Therefore it is no surprise to find that we have different ways in which we prefer to learn. Some people are more comfortable learning through practical activities and experience, others through a more reflective and theoretical approach, and still others from a mixture of both. Research has shown that some of us relate most effectively to a visual presentation of information, some to the spoken word and others learn effectively by imitation and practice.

Working out your learning preference

Have you worked out which way of learning works best for you? If not, one way is to think about the subjects you prefer and are motivated to do well in. Then begin to notice exactly what it is that encourages you to learn and enables you to remember, for instance:

- Do you enjoy subjects with a practical element?
- Do you enjoy revising and passing examinations?

- Do you enjoy the challenge of being given projects and assignments?
- Do you prefer to make notes from the information given you by the teacher, rather than find out the information in a more practical and active way?
- Do you prefer to discuss and work with others to find solutions rather than carrying out your own individual research?
- Are you comfortable with theories and facts?
- Do you like visual forms of information, like pictures and diagrams?
- Do you like verbal forms of information, like written and spoken explanations?

Note anything else that gives you clues about the way you gather and process information. Another way to find out your learning style is to identify which type of question you most frequently ask when faced with new information:

- **'Why?'** You need motivation to do things, for example how this course will relate to your interests or your future career.

- **'What?'** You need information from an expert source, for example presented in an organised and logical way with time for reflection.

- **'How?'** You need time to try things out and have feedback on what worked and what did not.

- **'What if . . .?'** You need to discover things for yourself, for example finding solutions to real problems.

You may find that you respond differently in different contexts, or that you have a similar response no matter what the subject being taught. Whatever you discover, it all helps to build up a picture of how you prefer to learn. This in turn helps you to take advantage of your natural skills and inclinations.

Teaching methods
It is not always possible for students to be taught solely according to their learning preferences. Some teachers present information through formal lectures, others encourage students to develop their analytical skills and discover solutions and facts for themselves. Teaching methods can often depend not only on the teacher but on the subject and the qualification.

It is in fact not always preferable to stick to only one learning style. For instance, employers prefer staff who are competent in gathering and processing information in the many different ways in which it is presented in the world of work. The best way for students to learn, therefore, is through a balance of teaching methods, so that they eventually become comfortable with a variety of learning styles.

Which type of course?

It may be that you are having difficulty deciding whether to do a vocational or academic course. Both appeal, both are possible and both lead eventually to the same goal. Having a clear idea of your learning preference can help in the decision-making. Generally, vocational courses leading to qualifications such as GNVQs, BTEC awards, NVQs or their Scottish equivalents, are taught in a more practical way than academic courses leading to A levels, AS levels or Scottish equivalents.

Assessment for vocational courses is characterised by project- and assignment-based work set throughout the course and external examinations. Students build up a portfolio (a record) of evidence of achievement. Academic courses are usually assessed mainly by a final examination, with considerable written work and study involved. Find out about the teaching methods used by asking teachers and course tutors specific questions about the way their subjects and courses are taught. Then it should be easier to make your decision, knowing which course will enable you to learn most easily.

Learning methods

How you prefer to learn affects the ease and speed at which you take in knowledge and understanding and at which therefore you gain qualifications and skills.

Knowing your learning style means you can identify where you are least comfortable and come up with strategies to ensure you still learn. For instance, if you know you learn best through a visual presentation of information and in fact are being taught through formal lectures, you can make your own notes and diagrams (even if there are handouts) to look at later; if you prefer to listen to the spoken word and are instead being given written information, why not try reading the information out loud to yourself – and recording it at the same time so that you have it there for future reference?; if you prefer to 'learn by doing', the very fact of making notes, using your hands to write your own words, will help.

DETERMINING YOUR OPTIONS

There are many different ways to qualify and train for a career working in the environment. Which one you choose will depend on a number of factors, including:

- for how long you wish to keep your options open (see below)
- the qualifications you have already
- the qualifications you expect to obtain
- the qualifications and training required for entry to particular careers
- how committed you are to a specific environmental career
- what is available and where
- how you prefer to learn
- which learning environment you prefer (school, college or work-based)
- your age (some careers have a minimum age entry requirement).

Taking account of some or all of the above will undoubtedly help in your decision-making process.

Keeping your options open

This is important to do if you are really unsure of your exact career direction. At school you can do it by choosing a broad range of subjects, encompassing both the sciences and the arts subjects; or by choosing academic rather than vocational subjects.

Degree level

At degree level, you can begin to narrow down your options by studying for a specific degree, such as oceanography, town planning, environmental health and so on, which commits you to a certain extent to a particular career area from the outset; or you can choose a more general degree such as geography, engineering, science, environmental studies, environmental sciences etc, which allows you to choose a specific career at a later stage. You can then either go directly into employment or choose to follow a postgraduate course of study in a specific area.

Options prior to gaining employment

The choices open to you whether you are in year 11, 12 or 13 at school or leaving college or university are:

- Going straight into employment (with or without training). It is obviously better for your career development if you are able to choose a job with some degree of opportunity for further training.

● Going on to a training programme (see below).

● Going on to further study (see below for details of the various qualifications and courses available). If you want to gain further qualifications at the end of year 11, it may be that one of the most important factors determining your options will be what courses are available locally. This is because living away from home is not usually a realistic option while you are under 18 years old.

Training programmes

National Traineeships
These are structured programmes of training designed by employers in a very wide range of industrial sectors for young people. Trainees are given the opportunity to work towards NVQ level 2 qualifications and may also gain other skills and qualifications. Many trainees are employed and earn a wage. Progression from a national traineeship can be to a **modern apprenticeship**, other employment or to further education. There is a national traineeship in environmental conservation being developed (at time of going to press this is not yet available in Scotland). Local careers offices and **TECs/LECs** will have details of what is available locally.

Modern apprenticeships
These are for young people from the age of 16 usually up to about 21 and are a work-based route to training and employment. They are now available in many industries and give apprentices the chance to learn a wide range of skills. The ones relevant to environmental work are:

● the modern apprenticeship in environmental conservation
● the modern apprenticeship in amenity horticulture or in countryside management (landscapes and ecosystems) as offered by the National Trust (see Chapter 4).

They are for people with the ability to gain high level skills and qualifications (up to NVQ level 3) and should not be seen as a soft option to A levels. Entry requirements are usually four GCSEs (A-C). The theory, skills and knowledge required can be very demanding. Modern apprentices are employees and as such earn a wage. The length of time on the programme is dependent on the abilities and needs of the apprentice. Your local TEC/LEC or careers office will have details of what is available in your area.

A level or graduate training programmes
Some employers may offer structured programmes of training for young people of higher than average ability. Your careers adviser will be able to give you information on what is available.

Options during employment
Employers do not always consider development of their staff as a priority. It is therefore often best to accept responsibility for your own career development in the first place. You will then be in control and can create your own opportunities to learn.

Becoming better skilled at your job or progressing to other posts can be achieved not only through time spent actually doing the job, but also by further study, either by specific courses or NVQs (see below). Find out what learning or training opportunities are available to you, by for example:

- looking at college prospectuses
- reading professional journals
- contacting your professional body
- reading 'finding out about the different courses' below
- identifying people inside and outside the organisation who may be able to help.

It is then important to discuss your training and career development plans with your employer. Consider how you can persuade or negotiate with your employer to take advantage of any learning or training opportunities you have identified.

On the job training
This is invaluable and forms part of everyone's daily work. It is work-based learning where you work alongside other people and learn exactly how to do certain tasks.

Off the job training
This is time spent away from the work place either at college, at a training centre, or with an outside training provider. It can take the form of short courses (from a single day up to a number of months) or formal education such as a college course leading to nationally recognised or

professional qualifications. Off the job training can be on a day- or block-release basis or as a secondment for, say, a year.

Distance learning
There may also be distance learning packages offered by colleges which may be relevant to your training needs and which may suit you better than attending a training course.

If you become unemployed

If you are aged between 18-24 and have been claiming Jobseekers Allowance for six months or more, you are eligible for the **New Deal**, a government initiative to get young people back to work or training. Following 'Gateway' (a series of steps to help you gain confidence, experience, develop skills and increase your employability), anyone who has not managed to find work has the opportunity of a place on one of the four New Deal options, one of which includes work with an environment task force (ETF) for up to six months. Some of the opportunities under ETF are to be found in:

- air pollution control
- water supply and waste water treatment
- environmental monitoring and instrumentation
- energy management
- contaminated land remediation
- environmental services
- marine pollution control
- renewable energy.

So even if you are unemployed, you can still have access to work and training in the environment!

THE DIFFERENT TYPES OF QUALIFICATION AVAILABLE POST-16

Environmentally specific (or related) qualifications can be important depending on the area in which you decide to work. However, experience or qualifications in another field along with an interest in environmental matters can also provide work opportunities within the environmental sector. For instance, environmental organisations all need a range of administrative, financial and personnel support.

All further education colleges and many secondary schools with sixth forms now offer a range of vocational and academic subjects. However, they do not all offer the same subjects or courses, so check with your teachers and careers adviser what is available in your area.

Vocational

Although vocational courses can and do lead on to further study, they train you for employment – specifically or generally, ie they enable you to learn about topics directly relevant to a particular career area or to the world of work in general. There are many different types available.

GNVQs/GSVQs

GNVQs and the Scottish equivalent GSVQs form a good basis for progression to employment, training or to further study. They give students (generally 16-19 year-olds in full-time education) basic skills in a vocational area as well as general skills in communication, numeracy and the use of computers. They can be studied alongside academic qualifications, such as GCSEs, A levels or equivalent.

They are available at three levels:

- *foundation* (level I in Scotland) which is roughly equal to four GCSEs at grades D-E or NVQ level 1 or Scottish equivalents

- *intermediate* (level II), roughly equal to four GCSEs at grades A-C, BTEC First award or NVQ level 2 or Scottish equivalents

- and *advanced* (level III), roughly equal to two A levels, BTEC National award or NVQ level 3 or Scottish equivalents.

They are offered in a broad range of vocational areas. The ones most relevant to environmentally related careers are the:

- intermediate and advanced level GNVQs in Land and Environment (England and Wales)
- levels II and III GSVQs in Land Based Industries.

The subjects covered include: natural resources of the land and environment, maintenance of ecosystems, environmental impact of industries, countryside recreation, landscape management and wildlife conservation. Advanced level GNVQs are becoming increasingly accepted by higher education institutions as entry to degree or diploma courses.

Other qualifications

BTEC awards (and the Scottish equivalent) are work-related and available in many different vocational areas at various levels. The ones relevant to environmental work include national and higher national diplomas and certificates in agriculture, horticulture and science. Options vary from college to college but may include conservation and wildlife management, forestry, countryside management, landscape design and rural studies.

City and Guilds and RSA also offer many different work-related qualifications, many of which are relevant to the environmental sector. It is possible to study these and BTEC awards full- or part-time. Employers value this type of qualification because it includes hands-on practical experience and enables students to learn additional skills such as communication and teamwork.

NVQs/SVQs

NVQs and the Scottish equivalent SVQs are not as broad-based as GNVQs but are specifically work-related, with competence at specific tasks being assessed in the work place or in simulated work environments, for example, at training centres or college. The emphasis is on practical skills not on passing examinations.

NVQs are made up of separate units covering different aspects of a job. You work towards the full NVQ (available at five different levels) by building up the various units of competence. You are assessed on your competence and skill at doing the job. Previous training or experience can also count towards an NVQ. You can choose from over 800 subjects covering almost every area of work. NVQs relating specifically to the environmental sector include Amenity Horticulture, Environmental Conservation (Landscapes and Ecosystems), Environmental Conservation (Archaeology), Forestry and Energy Management.

Academic

Academic (non-vocational) qualifications do not lead to a specific area of work. They are nonetheless extremely valuable as they can be the passport to further and higher education and employment, providing evidence of knowledge and ability to learn. They are also an alternative to vocational qualifications for those students who want to keep their options open before deciding on a particular career.

A levels/Highers

A levels are still the main entry qualification to higher education courses. In Scotland the equivalent, Highers, are being replaced in 1999/2000 by a new qualification, the Higher Still. Relevant subjects for

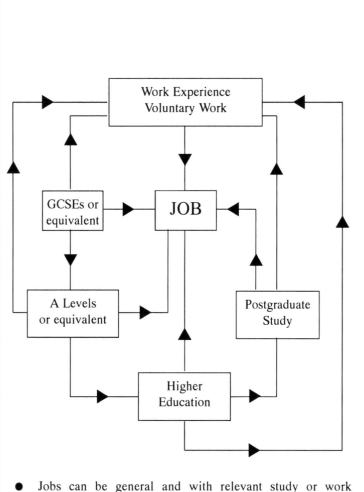

- Jobs can be general and with relevant study or work experience can become environmentally related.

- Higher education can involve specific or a more general degree. If a general degree, it is likely to be followed by environmentally relevant postgraduate study for a post in environmental work.

Fig. 8. Possible routes into environmental work.

environmentally related work, depending on what field you are particularly interested in, could be biology, botany, design and technology, geography, physics, mathematics and science.

AS levels
These are considered to be equal to half an A level. When combined with A levels or Advanced GNVQs, they are acceptable for entry to higher education courses.

HIGHER EDUCATION COURSES

A quick look through a compendium of degree course subjects reveals numerous courses related to the environmental sector (see Figure 9) even though the subject area is not always instantly recognisable as environmentally specific. Figure 9 takes only one example from each area. There are literally many hundreds of courses, all with the word 'environment' or similar, not necessarily in the subject area or course title but perhaps featuring in the course content. How on earth do you choose between them? It helps to take various factors into account, such as whether:

DEGREE COURSES

Subject area	Course title
agriculture	arboriculture and amenity forestry
town and country planning	countryside and environmental management
environmental and earth sciences	environmental science and agricultural ecology
engineering	environmental and ecological engineering
science	field biology and habitat management
architecture	environmental planning
geography	geography with environmental science
environmental health	environmental health sciences.

Fig. 9. Examples of degree course subjects and titles.

- you want to keep your options open a little longer
- you are interested in a particular aspect of the environment, such as conservation, environmental health, scientific research, etc
- a career area, such as engineering or science is your first interest and the environment is your second.

The course content gives crucial information when making a decision about which course to do. For instance, it has been said that environmental science courses cover the natural environment whereas environmental studies courses generally deal with the human, built environment (see Figure 10). However, there will always be exceptions. It is also true that most environmental science degree courses require A level sciences and environmental studies degree courses generally do not.

EXAMPLES OF COURSE CONTENTS

Environmental Science

Year 1: Global ecology and soil systems; atmosphere and oceans; geographic data acquisition; planet earth; earth surface processes; issues and techniques in environmental science; chemistry and the environment; microbial diversity; animals and plant physiology; ecology and evolution.

Years 2/3: Biometry; analytical science; issues and techniques in environmental science; chemical aspects of pollution; conservation; environmental law and assessment; soils; land utilisation and global environmental politics.

Environmental Studies

Year 1: Major environmental issues; skills and techniques for recording and communicating environmental information.

Year 2: Ecological, geological and climate systems; geographical pattern and processes; evolution of modern industrial society; population growth and population-resource issues.

Year 3: Optional studies of major environmental issues of local, national and global concern; management of environmental resources; individual research study.

Fig. 10. Examples of degree course titles.

If you really do not like science subjects or are not too good at them, it is important that you check the level of scientific knowledge expected or required on courses. You can always ask admissions tutors or someone already on the course. If you are concerned about your employment prospects post-degree, check out the destinations of past students – the university should be able to help you here. It could also be useful to check employers' opinions of a course if you want to be really sure. Careers advisers may be able to help you with this, as they have access to employers and knowledge of trends in the labour market. Read careers-related books (see Additional Resources) that give some indication of what employers are looking for in graduates.

Making it all count

The **Credit Accumulation and Transfer Schemes (CATS)** enables credit transfer between institutions. This means that it is easier for the learning you have achieved in one place to be recognised and applied elsewhere.

Most institutions offering degrees or other higher education qualifications in the UK now give credit values to their courses. Many courses are broken down into modules or units and each has a credit value. So you may build up a qualification by studying an appropriate number and combination of modules.

In addition short courses and development programmes run by employers can be CATS rated to enable them to contribute to a qualification at degree or postgraduate level. This way of crediting learning is sometimes called accreditation of prior learning (APL).

Benefits of credit transfer
Credit transfer is useful for many reasons, including the following:

● if you are transferring from one institution to another

● if you studied some years ago and now want to resume your study at another institution

● if you already hold a professional or other qualification for which you may be able to obtain credit towards another higher education course

● if you are working and studying and want some of your work experience to count towards your programme of study.

No qualifications? How to still get in to higher education
Access and foundation courses are designed for anyone over the age of 17 who wants to go on to higher education but does not yet have the necessary entry qualifications. They are usually one year in duration. Some are designed for entry to specific degrees while others are of a more general nature. Ask your careers adviser or local college for details of what is available.

OBTAINING FURTHER INFORMATION ABOUT ALL THE DIFFERENT COURSES

There are many ways to find out about courses related to the environmental sector. They include referring to:

● directories and careers encyclopaedias (see Additional Resources)

● computer databases, such as the UK Course Discover database which is the UK national database of 100,000 university and college courses produced by ECCTIS 2000 Ltd. It is available for access in most schools, colleges, universities and careers offices.

● professional bodies (such as the Environment Council, the Chartered Institute of Environmental Health, British Trust for Conservation Volunteers)

● careers advisers

● school, college and university prospectuses.

In addition, an organisation called Lantra (see Useful Addresses) handles enquiries relating to all land-based industry training, including agriculture, environmental conservation, horticulture, tree production and management. It was formed when The Environmental Training Organisation merged in April 1998 with other training organisations.

Other environmental training
Lots of organisations are offering environmental training and short courses, such as the following:

● The Institute of Ecology and Environmental Management runs a professional development programme offering low-cost training for ecologists and environmental managers. The training qualifies for structured continuous professional development (see below).

● British Trust for Conservation Volunteers offers practical conservation training courses.

● The Field Studies Council runs practical courses on a wide variety of subjects.

Having decided on the kind of training or qualifications you might be interested in having, you can then obtain more detailed information from the various sources quoted above (and refer to Useful Addresses and Additional Resources at the end of the book). If you are still unsure, refer back to the section on determining your options earlier in this chapter.

CONTINUOUS PROFESSIONAL DEVELOPMENT

One professional institution has defined **continuous professional development (CPD)** as:

'the systematic maintenance, improvement and broadening of knowledge and skills and the development of personal qualities necessary for the execution of professional and technical duties throughout a practitioner's working life.'

Increasingly professional institutes and associations require their members to maintain and improve their professional standards and keep up-to-date with developments in their profession. It is generally agreed that education and training is a continuing and lifelong process. Many profession have accepted the need for lifelong learning and are developing schemes which will help keep their members informed.

Reasons for CPD

There are two main reasons for CPD:

● To demonstrate that existing knowledge and skills are being regularly updated, in order to maintain a high degree of competency.

● To acquire new, relevant knowledge and develop more skills in order to keep up-to-date with developments in your field.

The pace of scientific, technological, social and political change is now so rapid and intense that an initial period of professional or vocational training often provides only the foundations of your knowledge and skills. Once you are qualified in your field, it is in many ways the beginning of your learning, not the end. Further development must take place if you are not only to remain up-to-date and competent in your field, but also to improve your skills and increase your knowledge. CPD can also be one of the best ways of progressing your career.

Examples of CPD

It is worth finding out what CPD is expected of you by your profession and how they will support you. People carry out CPD in a variety of ways, for example, through:

- postgraduate study
- distance learning
- short training courses (either in-house or via outside consultancies)
- reading the local and national press, professional journals
- learning from television or radio programmes
- exchanging ideas and information with colleagues
- working towards NVQs
- teaching others (helps with understanding).

The choice is wide. Make sure you know what training is on offer in your organisation and if there is nothing appropriate for you, check out where else or how else you could acquire more knowledge or improve your skills.

Evidence

Some professions expect their members to give evidence of their CPD. This may be by means of a portfolio, showing a personal record of your achievements and learning experiences. It is supposed to demonstrate the relationship between what you have learned and your competence in the job. A portfolio can also act as a morale or confidence booster in that it is a record of your successes.

CASE STUDIES

Keeping his options open

Alex was very good at maths, physics and chemistry and was thinking seriously of going into engineering as a career. However, in his spare time he was a member of his local Wildlife Trust and became more and more concerned about the effects of pollution on wildlife and habitats.

He could not make up his mind whether to commit himself to an engineering career or an environmental one. His careers adviser pointed out that maybe he could keep his options open a little longer by studying for a degree in chemical engineering with environmental management or with environmental protection. He chose the latter and after graduation managed to get a job with a chemical engineering company for whom he worked during his vacation. After a while, because of having researched pollution control and toxic waste management during his degree, he was well qualified when a vacancy came up for an environmental officer within the company. He now monitors his company's impact on the environment, looking at such matters as pollution levels, waste disposal and air emissions. 'It's great to have found a job that combines both my interests.'

Taking account of how we prefer to learn

Kim does not like school very much, finding studying for GCSEs harder than she would like. She prefers to be outdoors 'getting her hands dirty' rather than indoors 'learning from books'. Her careers teacher found out about the National Traineeships that would allow Kim to learn practical skills and yet also work towards a qualification. She hopes to start on one which leads to an NVQ level 2 in Maintaining and Conserving Rivers, Coasts and Waterways as soon as she leaves school. 'Knowing there is such an opportunity waiting for me has prompted me to make more of an effort at school as I won't have to be here for much longer.'

CHECKLIST

1.   Have you worked out your preferred learning style?

2.   Which factors will you take into account when deciding what route to take towards your chosen career?

3.   Ask what training you will get when you are applying for jobs.

4.   What resources will you use to find out about different courses and training opportunities?

5.   What evidence can you produce to show you are continuing your professional development?

6.   What provision will you make for your own ongoing education and training?

8
Studying Matters

CHOOSING WHAT TO STUDY

There is plenty of advice and information on how to make decisions about what you want to do in Chapters 5 and 7 of this book. If you have read them and carried out the various self-assessment activities suggested, you should by now have more focus in your thinking and be clearer about where you wish to go and what you want to study. If you are still uncertain, refer to those chapters again. Remember to:

- seek help and advice from teachers, careers adviser, family
- be realistic about your abilities – have contingency plans 'just in case'
- refer to directories, software, prospectuses for information
- look in your careers library for up-to-date information on careers in the environment (look under the careers library classification index references – for example, C for environmental health; Q for sciences and environmental science/studies; U for town and country planning, architecture and surveying; W for countryside management, forestry, agriculture).

CHOOSING WHERE TO STUDY

Once you know what you want to study, where to study becomes an easier choice. This is because you are then limited to what is available. For instance, if you want to go on to further education, most people attend the nearest college that offers the course. This is because of the obvious benefits of staying in the family home when you are still only 16. If your school offers the course you want to study and you want to stay at school, then your decision is easy. Choices have to be made when the course you want to study is offered by both school and college and you do not know which you would prefer.

Similarly, with higher education you may find that the course or subject you want to study is offered by a number of higher education institutions; or you may have a number of different courses on your list, all at different places. How do you choose between them?

Getting as much information as you can

Before you make any decision you need information. This is available in a number of formats.

Paper resources

Institutions produce prospectuses – booklets detailing not only the courses offered but also basic information about the institution itself, the accommodation and facilities available. There are also 'alternative' prospectuses, produced by students, which may give a slightly different angle to the information. Well worth reading. Look in your school or college careers library for copies or details of how to get hold of your own copy.

In addition there are a number of books and directories giving information about institutions. Refer to Additional Resources at the end of the book.

Videos and software

Many universities and colleges now produce their own videos or feature on CD-ROM, such as *Which? University*. Ask your careers teacher or careers adviser what videos and software are available in the careers library for you to refer to.

Visits

It is a very good idea to visit any institution on your shortlist, if it is at all possible. Many institutions have open days when potential students are invited to have a tour and meet the staff and students. Ensure you are ready for open days by preparing a list of questions in advance (see below) to ask. What do you need to know that would help you decide? Remember to ask students for their opinions. What made them choose the place? What do they still like about it? Are there any drawbacks?

Questions to ask

There are various factors you can take into account and questions you can ask which should help you move nearer to a decision, whether you are deciding between school and college or between higher education institutions:

● Which place would suit you best? If you are choosing between school and college, think about how you react to new places, new people – with excitement or fear?

- What facilities are available for learning, for leisure?
- What happened to past students? What career areas did they go into?
- What opportunities are there for you to have work experience or contact with employers?
- What subject options are available? Are they the ones you want?
- How are the subjects taught? (Remember your preferred learning style – Chapter 7.)
- What size are the classes? What opportunity is there for individual coaching? What is expected of you in terms of commitment?
- What kind of accommodation can you expect (and afford)?
- How easy is it to get to from the town, train or bus station?

Once you have found the answers to the above questions and related them to your own needs and desires, you are on the way to clarifying which institution(s) will suit you best.

Imagine being there

Finally, imagine being in one of the places on your shortlist. This will of course be easier if you have actually been there. If you have not been able to visit, refer to prospectuses or video so that you can begin to build up a picture in your mind's eye of you there, maybe walking from a lecture talking to people or sitting in the library studying. Does what you see look good to you? Does it sound as if it is the right place for you? Do you have a good feeling about it? Do this with each place you have chosen. Which ones score best?

FINANCING YOUR STUDIES AND TRAINING

If you are considering going on to further or higher education or into training, you will undoubtedly incur financial costs. Depending on your circumstances, whether you are living at or away from home, you may have to pay for your accommodation, food and drink. You will certainly have to pay for your books, course materials and leisure activities. In addition, you may have to find money for tuition and examination fees as well as transport costs.

> **Do not let financial considerations put you off going on to further study or training. There are all kinds of help available, including government loans for living costs at university or college.**

Although there will always be stories of students starting out their careers in debt, it is a fact that people with qualifications and training tend to be more employable than those without. This means that you should be able to repay any debts relatively quickly. If you take out a student loan, you will not be asked to pay it back until you earn at least £10,000, and then it will be in instalments, not in one lump sum. Most graduates' earning capacity is much higher than this.

See under Coping Strategies below for ways in which you can avoid getting into financial difficulties.

Starting to consider finance

This section gives a general outline of the new financial arrangements and support for students, representing government policy at the time of writing. Policies have a habit of changing so it is recommended that you obtain more specific information relevant to your particular situation and circumstances, before embarking on a course of study. You can contact the college or university where you are thinking of taking a course and/or the awards section of your local education authority (or the Student Awards Agency in Scotland and the Department of Education for Northern Ireland) in the first instance to find out if you are entitled to any financial support. Careers offices should also have up-to-date information.

Further education costs

Tuition fees
Tuition fees for further education are generally free to all UK students under 19 following a full-time course of study. Further education students, unlike those entering higher education, are not eligible for mandatory maintenance loans. Local education authorities (LEAs) may provide discretionary awards, although these are currently under review. If you are aged under 19, it is likely that your family will have to support you while you are studying.

Students aged 19 or over, or anyone studying part-time at any age, are usually expected to pay college tuition fees. However, many colleges do not charge any fees at all to full-time students. If you do not think you can afford fees, check out what financial help is available for potential students under Financial Help Available below.

Other fees and expenses
It is a good idea to ask colleges what their policy is on the payment of examination fees and registration fees before you start your course. You

will then be clear about exactly what you have to pay or contribute towards. In addition, you may wish to consider how much you need to pay for your books, any equipment, other study materials or extras such as field trips. Course tutors or admission tutors should be able to give you some indication of costs in these areas.

Transport costs
Some further education students receive help with the cost of transport from their home to school or college. Ask the awards section of your local education authority what help they will give you towards your transport expenses. Usually LEAs help with transport expenses only to your nearest college offering the course you want to do. For instance, if you want to study amenity forestry and it is only offered at an agricultural college some distance away from your home, you may still be able to receive some financial help towards your travel expenses. However, if the course you want is also offered at a college nearer to you, you will almost certainly have to go to the nearer college to receive travel expenses. Some LEAs do not offer any financial help at all with travel expenses.

Training costs
If you are taken on as a modern apprentice or national trainee on an employed basis, you will receive a wage from your employer. If not, you will receive a training allowance, as for any TEC- or LEC-funded course.

Higher education costs
The government changed the way higher education courses are funded with new financial support arrangements from 1st September 1998.

Tuition fees
From 1998/99 new entrants to higher education have to pay up to a maximum of £1,000 a year towards tuition fees. There is no loan available from the government for this. The actual amount payable will depend on the income of the student or the student's family. Because of this, some students with low incomes will not be able to make a contribution to tuition fees and will have to apply to their local education authority for help. The tuition fee does not apply to postgraduate teacher training (PGCE) courses.

Maintenance grants
From 1999/2000 students are no longer entitled to a maintenance grant

but have to apply annually for a maintenance loan to help pay their living costs. You do not have to pay back the loan while you are studying. Repayment of the loans will usually be collected by your employer and will not begin until you earn over £10,000 per annum. Generally, all higher education full-time courses attract loans. Specifically, in order to be eligible for loans, your course must lead to one of the following qualifications:

- a first degree, such as a BA, BSc or BEd
- a Diploma of Higher Education (DipHE)
- a Higher National Diploma (HND)
- a Postgraduate Certificate of Education (PGCE) or other postgraduate course or initial teacher training leading to the award of qualified teacher status or equivalent
- an NVQ at level 4 where it is awarded along with a first degree, DipHE or HND.

Access or conversion courses for higher education access are not eligible for loans. For the full story on the new financial arrangements, read *Supporting Students in Higher Education* published by the Department for Education and Employment (see Additional Resources).

Transferring courses
If you are unhappy with your choice of course and wish to transfer to another one (see case study at end of chapter), it is important that you make arrangements to do this *before* you leave your current course, or your financial support may be affected.

FINANCIAL HELP AVAILABLE

For whatever reason you may need some help with financing your study or training. The following lists some of the help currently available. Your careers officer or teachers may know of other sources of help.

Transport expenses
As mentioned above, full-time students, aged 16-18 in further education, may be able to get help with their transport costs to and from college. Contact the awards section of your local education authority for details.

Access funds
Colleges and universities receive funds (**access funds**) from the government to help those students who are really struggling to get by

financially and whose access to higher education could therefore be denied. Students fulfilling certain criteria may receive these funds and, if necessary, hardship loans to help then begin or continue their studies. It is up to the colleges and universities to decide who receives the financial help and how much to give. Contact your student union welfare office for details in the first instance.

Benefits
You or your family may be entitled to housing or some kind of income-related benefit. Contact your local Benefits Agency for details.

Career development loans
These help people aged 18 or over pay for vocational education or training by giving deferred repayment, interest free bank loans. The loan is for up to two years for any full-time, part-time or distance-learning course that is job-related. It ranges from £300 to £8,000 and pays for up to 80 per cent of course fees, books, childcare and, for full-time students only, living expenses. Contact 0800 585 505 (Monday to Friday, 9am - 9pm) for more information and details of how to apply. Information leaflets are also available from jobcentres, careers offices, TECs/LECs and colleges.

Sponsorships, grants and bursaries
A charitable trust may be able to give you a grant or bursary to enable you to continue your studies. Similarly, an employer may give you financial support and practical training while you study for a work-related qualification. If you are interested in this kind of support, there are several things you can do:

- Talk to your careers teacher or careers adviser for information.
- Obtain information from the careers library in school or college about organisations and charities offering sponsorships, grants or bursaries.
- Write to any organisation in which you are interested.
- Refer to books such as *Sponsorship for Students, The Educational Grants Directory* or the *Directory of Grant Making Trusts* (see Additional Resources).

Individual Learning Accounts
These are a new initiative from the government, as part of the lifelong learning agenda to support individual learning. The aim is to give people the chance to choose what and how they want to learn and to encourage

them to save and plan for learning. A number of projects, developed by TECs in England and Wales, are testing out different approaches to establishing individual learning accounts (ILAs) and to encouraging people to use them. Projects are likely to include methods of providing people with access to credit (for example, in the form of bank loans) for their learning-related expenditure. Ask your local TEC for details.

Jobseekers Allowance
If you are unemployed and studying part-time you may be entitled to receive Jobseekers Allowance. Ask your local jobcentre for details, particularly about the New Deal initiative where there is specific provision for those who wish to study to improve their employability.

Tax relief
You can claim tax relief on payments for work-related training which counts towards an NVQ/SVQ up to and including level 5. Any unit or part of a unit of an NVQ/SVQ can qualify for tax relief. Tax relief is also given for GNVQs/GSVQs. Consult the Inland Revenue leaflet IR119 Tax Relief for Vocational Training for more detailed information (see Additional Resources).

Lower priced goods
Universities and colleges often have campus shops offering food, drinks, stationery and other goods at lower prices than high street shops. There are also bookshops which usually have a stock of secondhand course books.

COPING STRATEGIES

What can you do if you find you are:

- Struggling to cope with the amount of work?
- Finding some classes too difficult?
- Missing your family/girlfriend/boyfriend/friends?
- Finding it hard to live on a tight budget?
- Unsure whether you want to carry on with environmental science, the national traineeship or whatever course or training you are doing?

Talking about it
The important thing is to talk to someone about any problems as soon as possible. The old maxim 'a trouble shared is a trouble halved' is very

true. Simply talking things through with a sympathetic listener can help immensely. You may also get a different perspective on the problem. The solution to your problem could be easy seen from someone else's point of view, whether it is arranging for extra tuition, talking through your options or seeking financial support. Do not wait until the problem is too big to handle. Build up your own support network of friends, family, tutors and lecturers – people you can call on when you need to and who will look out for you. You may want to do the same for someone else.

It's your choice
Remember that how you respond to a situation is your choice. You can choose to be miserable or you can choose to do something about your misery. It has been said that opportunities are sometimes missed because they can be disguised or viewed as crises.

It is always possible to look at a situation another way. For instance, you could find a subject impossibly difficult and want to give it up at the first hurdle or you could decide to look on it as a challenge and first find ways of meeting the challenge. What you have to decide is what is best for you at any one time. Or ask someone else to help you review your options.

Knowing your resources
Gather as much information as possible so you know where to go for help and support should you need any. For instance, do you know where to go if you have money troubles? If you are falling behind with your work? If you are just feeling unhappy for no particular reason? Find out what resources are on hand to help you before you need them.

Thinking outside the box
Have a look at the puzzle in Figure 11. Have you managed to do it? If you have, you will know that the solution lies in being creative and 'thinking outside the box' (if you have not managed to find an answer, see page 126).

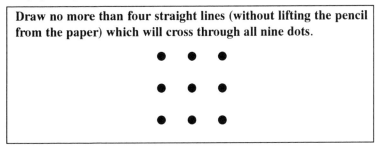

Draw no more than four straight lines (without lifting the pencil from the paper) which will cross through all nine dots.

Fig. 11. Puzzle.

It helps to gain a wider perspective and see outside and beyond any problem. There is never only one solution. What other options are open to you? What advice would you give to someone in your position? Brainstorm ideas, no matter how silly they might at first seem. Ask friends to help. For instance, if lack of money is the problem, how many different ways can you think of for saving or earning some money? Once you have a list of different options, look at each one critically and realistically to see which are feasible and which are not.

TACTICS TO USE IN POTENTIAL PROBLEM AREAS

Changing direction

Whatever decisions you make, it is often a good idea to have contingency plans or alternative ideas ready for when things do not work out as planned. For instance, you may get better grades than expected, you may not get the grades you need to do the subject or course you want or your ideas may simply change. Having already thought of alternatives makes it easier to change direction.

The workload

Get into good habits from the start and structure your time. Use a diary or weekly worksheet, noting when each piece of work is due and how long you need to do it. Write in when you will allocate time on it. You can then see immediately if you are falling behind schedule. That is the time to ask for extensions, not on the due date!

It is very important to get yourself organised before you start your studies or training. You will certainly build up piles of lecture notes and handouts. What system will you use to store them? It is vital to be able to find your notes and read them in a logical order when you need to revise. Numbering and dating notes is a good habit to develop. What will you use to file your paper in? As anyone reading this book is bound to be environmentally friendly, it is highly likely that recycling old envelopes or using cardboard boxes from the supermarket will be high on the list for filing papers. This also has the added advantage of saving money.

Ask yourself continuously 'Am I working effectively?' 'Will I be able to understand my notes after a period of time?' Consider the most useful way for you to take notes and learn.

Learning maps
Many people use the traditional method of linear note-making learnt at school; others use versions of learning maps or nuclear note-making.

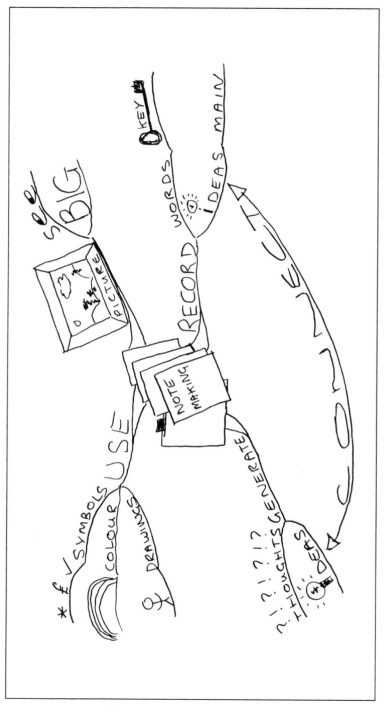

Fig. 12. Example of a learning map.

This method of note-making is often based on the technique of 'Mind Mapping'® (registered trademark of the Buzan Organisation used with permission), developed by Tony Buzan. The point is to make a visual representation of notes, working from a central topic or subject outwards in all directions, capturing key words and using colours and drawings. Such maps enable you not only to record a great deal of information on only one page but also to make associations – connections – between the ideas (see Figure 12) and to see the big picture, literally. If you wish to use less paper and save trees, this latter method is the obvious one to master. See Additional Resources and Useful Addresses for details of Tony Buzan's book on the subject of Mind Mapping and the Buzan Centres.

Learning from mistakes
Remember that it is always possible to learn from so-called mistakes. If you did not do as well as you thought, do you now know how you can do better next time? What have you learnt from the result you achieved?

Money

What does it really cost to go on to further or higher education or training? Ask current students how they cope and what things cost. Find out from your chosen institution what you are expected to pay in terms of tuition fees, examination fees, course materials and so on. If you find out information in advance, you may be able to build up your funds before you start your course.

A budget is essential if you are not to get into financial difficulties. Work out how much money you need for essentials such as living expenses, food and books. Anything left over after buying the essentials is yours to have fun with or put aside for emergencies. Some students take a year out and earn money to finance their future studies or training. Others take a part-time job while they are studying. This is fine, so long as it does not interfere with your studies by taking too much of your time, strength and energy.

Finding help
Remember: ask for help as soon as you need it not when the problem is too big to handle. Student counsellors, welfare officers, careers advisers, tutors, teachers and family are all there to support you. Use them.

Health

It is sometimes easy to ignore the importance of caring for your health when you are busy studying or having fun. However, if you wish to be successful in your studies, you also need to stay healthy. This means a good diet, plenty of exercise, sufficient sleep and regular breaks between study periods. If you are struggling with an essay or assignment, it can pay to take a break. Think about the situations when you suddenly come up with an idea or remember something important – it is usually when you least expect it and usually when you are doing something restful or different to the task in hand. Breaks enable your brain to take time to integrate ideas and assimilate experiences and come up with solutions to problems. Give it the chance to do so.

CASE STUDIES

Deciding for himself

Peter wanted to do A levels and could do them at his school or at his local college. 'My brother had done his A levels at college successfully so I thought I would follow in his footsteps. Then I really thought about what it would be like. Most of my friends were staying on at school and I knew all the teachers. School was also easier to get to than college.' Peter talked to his family about it. 'My brother is actually very different from me and didn't enjoy school, so couldn't wait to leave to go to college. I decided to stay at school and am now coming to the end of my first year of studies. I'm really glad I chose to stay here. I'll be ready to leave at the end of next year but for the time being I'm enjoying school life.'

Opting for change

Laurel is in her second year at university, enjoying studying for a degree in Ecology, Conservation and Environment. She was not always as happy. Her first choice was a degree in Chemistry, Resources and the Environment. 'It was OK, but I wasn't really comfortable with it. I had enjoyed sciences at school and always done particularly well in chemistry, but this was entirely different. I realised I didn't enjoy it as much as I thought. I then met someone at a party who was on the Ecology, Conservation and Environment course and it sounded much more what I wanted to do.' So Laurel talked to her tutors and was advised to go home for the weekend to discuss things with her family. She then changed courses mid-term in her first year, before too much time had passed. 'I'm so glad I decided to change. I still use my chemistry but in a less concentrated way. I am now much more motivated to learn as I am enjoying my course more.'

CHECKLIST

1. What are your options for courses or training?

2. Write down your reasons for your choices of course or training.

3. What motivates you most about studying or training?

4. What appeals to you about any particular institution?

5. Do you know who to turn to for help and advice?

6. What resources will you use to help you make decisions?

7. How many places can you visit before you decide on one in particular?

8. Have you the motivation and determination to succeed despite any obstacles?

9. What are your contingency plans or alternative ideas?

9
Taking the Next Step

REVIEWING AND PLANNING

It is often useful when planning the next step to review all the information gathered to date. This enables you to recognise how far you have come, to acknowledge any decisions you have made and to identify any gaps in your knowledge.

Looking back
Refer back to any relevant chapters in this book to help you review where you are now in your career decision-making.

Career direction
Chapter 5 suggests you start a 'career direction record', noting any information you gather about yourself and any career ideas you have. It is a good idea to examine such a record regularly, as you and your ideas change from time to time.

If you are still unsure about your skills and abilities, go back over this chapter and re-do the exercises which give you clues about yourself and the type of work which would suit you.

Environmental jobs
If you want to refresh your memory about the huge variety of environmental jobs available, refer to Chapters 2-4. Remember to list any jobs that interest you and give reasons for your choices. This helps you identify what motivates you.

Environmental courses and training
Chapter 7 gives information on the courses and training available in the environmental sector. It outlines the initial steps to becoming skilled and qualified, and also identifies how you can maintain and update your skills for lifelong development. Have you noted which courses or training programmes interest you?

ACTION PLAN

Current career direction idea.................(date)................

Alternatives..

Information needed to help me towards my goal (eg qualifications, training, salary, nature of work, opportunities)

....

....

....

What else do I have to do to make myself more employable? (eg voluntary work, membership of societies, subscription to journals or magazines)

....

....

....

Resources to use (specific people, books, magazines, videos, software)

....

....

....

Next steps

I will find out about.............................by (date)...........

I will refer to ....by (date)...........

I will talk to ....by (date)...........

I will visit..by (date)...........

I will join ....by (date)...........

I will..by (date)...........

Fig. 13. Example of an action plan.

Looking forward

An important stage of planning is the action plan (see example in Figure 13). This is a written record of what you are going to do next to help you move towards your goal. Its aim is to focus and clarify your thoughts and ideas. It is hoped that you will be motivated to take action by seeing clearly what needs to be done specifically and by when. It also acts as a record of what you have done – a reminder of your achievements to date.

You could expand or adapt your action plan to include comments about the information you find out. For instance, having found out about the nature of the work, do you still want to do it? If you do not, what is it that has made you change your mind? This could be useful information to record, so that you know more clearly what you want in the future.

When thinking of the resources available to you, remember to note down not just books and videos, but also any people who may be useful, such as careers advisers, careers teachers and family.

BEING PREPARED

The Boy Scouts' motto is a good one to adopt. Staying one step ahead of the opposition means being prepared. There is much that you can do in advance of applying for jobs and courses and going for interviews.

Application forms

Application forms are all very similar (see example in Figure 14), asking you basic information such as the following:

- personal information (name, address, date of birth) – some organisations also ask for marital status and most now ask for ethnic background (for equal opportunity monitoring)
- educational achievements (schools/colleges attended, examination results and dates)
- work history or experience
- interests and hobbies.

You can prepare all of this in advance and have it ready in your 'career direction record' to refer to as and when necessary. It will save you time.

Additional information

Most forms have a space which asks you for additional information. This may be in the form of a question, such as 'Why are you applying

Groundwork Application Form

Action for the Environment

Please complete this in your own handwriting in black ink.

Surname	Forenames
Address	Home telephone Work telephone
For what position are you applying?	Source of Application (Personal reference, Newspaper etc.)

EDUCATION

Please give details of your full time education since the age of 15.

Dates		Name of School/College/University	Examination taken. Give subjects, dates, and, if passed Grade. Diploma, Certificates awarded.
From	To		

Please give details of any business courses attended and qualification, if any achieved.

Date	Place and type of course	Qualifications

Fig. 14. Example of an application form.

118

for this job/course?' or an instruction, such as 'Outline your relevant skills and experience.' Whatever the type of question or instruction, the information required is similar. The employer or course provider wants to know your motivation for applying.

What you write here shows the recruiter whether you have done your homework and worked out how you could fit in and contribute to the organisation or how the course would benefit you. This is your opportunity to sell yourself. Although you cannot write it all in advance, you can record your strengths, skills and experience, so that you have the information to hand and ready to adapt to any particular opportunity.

References
Some application forms ask for references. Think now who you can use. You will almost certainly need two references, usually one academic (for example, a teacher or tutor) and one from the world of work (a current or previous employer, maybe from work experience or a part-time job). These are people who will be asked about your character, personality and ability. Make a note of their names and addresses. Make sure you ask anyone first if they will agree to being your referee before including them on a form. Do not leave it until the deadline approaches for sending off the form. If you tell them at the beginning that you are making several applications and ask them if you can use them as referees, you will not have to contact them each time.

Remember to keep copies of any application forms you complete. Not only will you need them to revise for any interviews, but they are also useful for reference when you have to fill in other application forms.

Curriculum Vitae (CV)
Some organisations ask for CVs instead of application forms and, if you are making speculative enquiries, it is usual to send your CV with a covering letter. A CV is basically a 'story of your life' – a summary of your qualifications, experience and interests. It is useful to prepare one in advance, remembering to update or adapt it as and when required. The information will be very similar to that required on an application form (see above). The format will almost certainly be different, as it is up to you how you present the information. It is a good idea to fit everything on to one or two sides of A4 paper. Ask your careers teacher or careers adviser for help in compiling your CV. Make sure that it is typed and that you use good quality paper.

Interviews
There is an enormous amount you can do to prepare yourself in advance

for an interview. While in education or training, take up any and every opportunity to have interview practice. You may find that employers, careers advisers and training providers all offer to help prepare students for interviews. Find out what is available to you. If there is nothing on offer when you want it, ask a friend or a member of your family to role play interviewer/interviewee with you. If you cannot find anyone to play the part of the interviewer, play that part and the interviewee yourself. The important thing is how you answer the questions.

Making a video
Video yourself if at all possible. This enables you to see clearly if you have any annoying habits. For example, do you fidget too much, do you gesture too much with your hands? Do you mumble? Are you slouching? If you cannot get hold of a video camera, maybe you could record yourself on audio tape. This will at least enable you to review critically your answers to questions. Are you too monosyllabic or too talkative? What is the tone and pitch of your voice like? Is it interesting or boring to listen to?

Preparing answers
If you are having difficulty in answering some questions, put yourself in the interviewer's shoes. What would you want to hear to persuade you to take this person (you) on? Interviewers usually want to know four things:

● Your motivation for applying (what interests you).
● Your commitment (what homework you have done on the organisation, course or place, your enthusiasm, your career ideas).
● Your ability to do the course or job (your skills, achievements and experience).
● Your personality (will you fit in?).

You can begin to consider now how you would respond to any questions about the above. For instance, what are your career goals, your strengths and your achievements? What evidence can you give for any strengths you believe you have? Where did you demonstrate them? And how?

Being prepared
Most interviewers ask questions designed to find out your weaknesses or limitations. Think about these in advance. What could you improve on in your skills and experience? What have you learnt from any so-called mistakes?

If you systematically work through the above guidelines, you will be giving yourself a better chance of success in any interview you have, by being well prepared and well rehearsed.

INCREASING YOUR CHANCES

Showing commitment and enthusiasm

Employers and course providers are impressed if you can demonstrate that you have carried out some research about the organisation or the course beforehand. This shows you are motivated and keen and may give you the edge on other applicants who may not be so thorough. Careers offices and libraries often have valuable information that can help you in your research. Refer to the Useful Addresses and Additional Resources at the end of the book.

Chapter 6 gives suggestions on how to demonstrate your commitment to work in the environment. Ideas include voluntary work, membership of local environmental organisations and ways of keeping yourself up-to-date with current environmental issues.

Job advertisements can be an important source of information. They show the trends in the types of jobs available.

Keeping up-to-date
A knowledge of environmental issues is useful when you are looking for a job or a course and will also stand you in good stead at interview. Chapter 1 will help in this respect as it identifies the various concerns current at the time of writing. However, it is important to ensure that your knowledge is up-to-date. Keep in touch with recent developments by reading relevant magazines and journals. The national press, television and radio can also provide useful information by way of news items or features and documentaries.

Looking in the right place for vacancies

There are many different places to look for vacancies:

- Advertisements in the national press (*The Guardian* on a Wednesday features environmental posts), or local newspapers, professional journals and magazines (refer to Additional Resources).
- Private employment or recruitment agencies (one specialising in environment jobs is Evergreen Resources, Unit D, Telford Road, Basingstoke, Hants RG21 2YU. Tel: 01256 332220).
- Careers offices.

- Jobcentres.
- The Countryside Management Association (see Useful Addresses) runs a jobs advice network on subscription, which includes weekly bulletins of job vacancies, some of which may not have been advertised elsewhere.

> **However, research has found that only one out of five vacancies is advertised.**

This means that if you only look in the above places for employment opportunities, you could be missing out. Make sure you also use some of the following proactive ways of finding work:

- Talk to other people – family members, friends, people in the community, staff at careers offices, school, college. Remember the importance of networking outlined in Chapter 6? Ask anyone who can help 'Do you know of any organisations I could contact?'

- Contact any organisation that interests you, whether you know they have a vacancy or not. Use *Yellow Pages* for local contacts or the Addresses section at the end of this book for national contacts. Tell them about your skills, experience and interests and why you would benefit their organisation. Do your research on the organisation first, so you know where you would fit in. Ask if they would be willing to meet you to discuss any possible opportunity for you to prove your worth. If you are really interested, you may want to suggest working for them on a voluntary basis for a period, so they can assess you at no cost to them.

- Consider voluntary or part-time work in an organisation. As discussed in Chapter 6, this enables you to 'get your foot in the door' and be in the right place at the right time should any full-time, permanent vacancies come up.

Using more than one of the above methods will increase your chances of finding work.

Job specification

Organisations often send out job specifications or job descriptions with application forms. It is important to read these carefully and match any skills or experience required to what you have. The skill then is to evidence those skills and experience in your application. How can you prove you are 'good at organising', that you have 'excellent interpersonal skills' or that you 'care for the environment'? What activities have you engaged in or do you currently do that demonstrate these attributes?

Make sure that you can back up every statement you make. If you cannot think of any instance where you have demonstrated a skill or quality, ask a friend or a member of your family if they can remember a time when you did so. Two heads are usually better than one.

LEARNING FROM SETBACKS

We do not always get what we want when we want it. One of the hardest things about applying for courses or jobs is coping with rejection. Sales people cope with this by believing that every 'no' is one step nearer to a 'yes', based on the law of averages. This is good positive thinking which always helps, but you could enhance your chances even further by the following.

Doing something different

If you are continually being turned down for jobs, ask someone (for example, a careers adviser) to look at your application form, your CV, your interview technique. Review your job- or course-finding strategy – are you going for the ones most appropriate to your interests, skills and attributes?

Obtaining feedback

Interviewers will sometimes, if asked, tell you how you appeared to them and what gaps there were in your knowledge, experience or abilities. Make a note of this and decide how you can improve for next time. If you are not even making it to the interview stage, again take a fresh look at your application form or CV and obtain someone else's opinion on it.

Giving yourself some feedback too

Make a note immediately after an interview of as many as you can remember of the questions that were asked of you and the answers you gave. What worked well or not so well? What would you do differently? How could you improve on your performance? Be honest with yourself and ask someone else for their opinion too. File your notes for future reference.

FINAL MESSAGES

● Keep going – view difficulties as challenges.

● If there is something you really want to do, continue to find ways of doing it.

● Be flexible and prepared to adapt to changing circumstances.

● Learn from every experience.

● Make the most of every situation.

● While waiting to be accepted for a job or course, remember that you can still pursue your interest in the environment by being involved in green activities, whether on a voluntary or paid work basis.

● Enjoy the journey as well as the destination!

CASE STUDIES

Feeling more confident

Jon is looking for a job as an environmental health officer. After various attempts, he has never got further than the first interview. He began to feel low and dejected. Then a friend suggested he review his whole strategy. 'She said that if what I was doing wasn't working, which it obviously wasn't, why didn't I do something different. So I contacted one of my referees, an employer I had had a work placement with, and asked if he would give me some interview practice. He was only too pleased. I also tape-recorded the interview so I could not only review the answers I gave but also how I came over.' Jon's referee gave him some suggestions as to how he could improve his interview technique and Jon is now feeling more confident about his next interview.

On the way to employment

Meera decided to enhance her job search by sending off speculative letters with her CV to various environmental organisations in which she was interested. 'I looked through *Yellow Pages* and then asked their personnel offices for any company brochures, for background information. I also made sure I obtained the name of the personnel officer, so I could write to someone specific within the organisation.' She followed up each letter with a telephone call and eventually one organisation wanted to know more about her. She managed to negotiate a temporary work placement with them which 'gives me the opportunity to see what they're like as well as them being able to see if I can do the work.' Meera hopes that even if this job does not lead to a permanent one with the same company, the work experience gained will help with future applications.

Using available resources

Charlie decided to make use of the resources available to him while on his training programme in amenity horticulture. The college where he goes one day a week was offering to help people with CV writing. Charlie now has a professional looking CV, which he can adapt as and when necessary. ' I initially wanted to put in everything I had ever done, whether it was relevant or not. The careers adviser not only helped me to be more selective but also helped me to identify my key skills.'

CHECKLIST

1. Review what you have learnt about yourself and jobs in the environment (refer to previous chapters as necessary).

2. Have you completed an action plan yet?

3. What additional information will you give on an application form?

4. Have you produced a CV which you can adapt to different job applications?

5. Have you identified at least two people who will write references for you?

6. Do you know who can help you with interview practice?

7. What are your main strengths? And what can you do to be even better?

8. How will you cope if you do not get the job you want when you want it?

9. Are you enjoying the journey as well as the destination?

Appendix

The solution to the puzzle on page 109, in which you were asked to draw four straight lines without lifting the pencil from the paper, crossing through all nine dots.

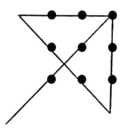

No one said you could not go outside the 'box' of dots or that you had to draw through the centre of each dot!

Glossary

Access funds. Government money given to colleges and universities to help students in serious financial difficulty.

BTEC awards. Work-related qualifications awarded by the Edexcel Foundation. The Scottish equivalents are awarded by the Scottish Qualifications Authority.

Career Direction Record. Your personal record of careers information relevant to you.

Credit Accumulation and Transfer Scheme (CATS). Enables the learning undertaken in one institution to be recognised and credited in another.

Career Development Loans (CDLs). Deferred repayment bank loans to help individuals pay for vocational training they otherwise could not afford.

Core skills. Skills which are common requirements by employers, eg communication, numeracy, information technology, teamwork, problem solving.

Continuous Professional Development (CPD). The maintenance and improvement of skills, standards and knowledge in a career.

Curriculum Vitae (CV). A summary of personal details, interests and employment experience which is sometimes sent to employers instead of an application form.

DfEE. The Department for Education and Employment.

GNVQ/GSVQ. General National Vocational Qualifications and the Scottish equivalent General Scottish Vocational Qualifications are vocational qualifications for 16-19 year-old students.

Individual Learning Accounts (ILAs). Part of the government's lifelong learning agenda; these are being established to encourage people to save and plan for learning.

Lantra. An organisation which handles enquiries for all land-based industry training.

Learning Direct. A freephone advice line for adults funded by the DfEE, giving callers access to advice on learning. Freephone 0800 100 900.

127

Learning style/preference. How people learn best. We all have different ways of processing information and understanding.

Lifelong learning. The concept that learning is a continuous process, with individuals being able to access learning opportunities throughout life, rather than once only at school or college.

Local Agenda 21. An initiative to encourage local governments to take action on green issues at a local level, involving businesses, communities and individuals.

Modern Apprenticeship. A work-based route to employment via a programme for young people (usually aged 16–21) combining practical training with theoretical knowledge. Trainees can work towards NVQ level 3 qualifications.

National Traineeship. A work-based training programme for young people combining practical training with theoretical knowledge. Trainees can work towards NVQ level 2.

New Deal. A government initiative to improve employment prospects for young unemployed people.

NVQs/SVQs. National Vocational Qualifications and the Scottish equivalent Scottish Vocational Qualifications are specifically work-related qualifications which are usually assessed in the work place.

Sustainable development. Not taking out more of the earth's natural resources than can be replaced naturally.

TECs/LECs. Training and Enterprise Councils (England and Wales) and Local Enterprise Companies (Scotland): government funded agencies responsible for coordinating government training and enterprise projects in regional areas.

Transferable skills. Skills which are not specific to any one job but which can be adapted to suit different working environments.

UK Course Discover. A database of university and college courses, produced by ECCTIS 2000 Ltd.

Vocational. Work-related.

Youth for Britain database. A database of volunteer opportunities for young people aged between 16 and 25. Available in many careers offices, schools and colleges as part of the ECCTIS 2000 UK Course Discover database.

Useful Addresses

CAREERS ADVICE

Careers offices – look under 'careers' in your local telephone directory.

ENVIRONMENTAL ORGANISATIONS

British Trust for Conservation Volunteers, 36 St Mary's Street, Wallingford, Oxfordshire OX10 0EU. Tel: (01491) 839766. Fax: (01491) 839646. Email: information@btcv.org.uk Website: http://www.btcv.org.uk

The Chartered Institute of Environmental Health, Chadwick Court, 15 Hatfields, London SE1 8DJ. Tel: (0171) 928 6006. Fax: (0171) 827 5865. Email: cieh@dial.pipex.com Website: http://www.cih.org.uk

Council for Environmental Education, University of Reading, London Road, Reading RG1 5AQ. Tel: (0118) 975 6061. Fax: (0118) 975 6264. Email: info@cee.i-way.co.uk

Countryside Commission, John Dower House, Cheltenham GL50 3RA. Tel: (01242) 521381. Fax: (01242) 584270. Email: info@countryside.gov.uk Website: http://www.countryside.gov.uk

The Countryside Management Association, Administration, Drury Lane, Knutsford, Cheshire WA16 6HB. Write for information about jobs advice network and how to subscribe to magazine.

Earthwatch Institute, 57 Woodstock Road, Oxford OX2 6HJ. Tel: (01865) 311600. Fax: (01865) 311383. Email: info@uk.earthwatch.org Website: http://www.earthwatch.org

English Nature, Northminster House, Peterborough PE1 1UA. Tel: (01733) 455100. Fax: (01733) 455103. Email: enquiries.en.nh@gtnet.gov.uk Website: http://www.english-nature.org.uk

The Environment Agency, Rio House, Waterside Drive, Aztec West, Almondsbury, Bristol BS12 4UD. Tel: (01454) 624400. Website: http://www.environment-agency.gov.uk

Environment Council, 21 Elizabeth Street, London SW1W 9RP. Tel: (0171) 824 8411. Fax: (0171) 730 9941. Email:

environment.council@ukonline.co.uk Website:
http://www.greenchannel.com/tec Produces *habitat*, *Directory of Environmental Courses*.

Environmental Law Foundation, Suite 309, 16 Baldwins Gardens, Hatton Square, London EC1N 7RJ. Tel: (0171) 404 1030. Fax: (0171) 404 1032.

The Forestry Commission, Personnel Dept, 231 Corstorphine Road, Edinburgh EH12 7AT. Tel: (0131) 334 0303. Fax: (0131) 314 6174. Website: http://www.forestry.gov.uk

Friends of the Earth, 26-28 Underwood Street, London N1 7JQ. Tel: (0171) 490 1555. Fax: (0171) 490 0881. Email: info@foe.co.uk Website: http://www.foe.co.uk

Greenpeace, Personnel Department, Canonbury Villas, Islington, London N1 2PN. Tel: (0171) 865 8100. Fax: (0171) 865 8200. Email: info@uk.greenpeace.org Website: http://www.greenpeace.org.uk

Groundwork National Office, 85-87 Cornwall Street, Birmingham B3 3BY. Tel: (0121) 236 8565. Fax: (0121) 236 7356. Email: info@groundwork.org.uk Website: http://www.groundwork.org.uk

The Institute of Ecology and Environmental Management, 36 Kingfisher Court, Hambridge Road, Newbury, Berkshire RG14 5SJ. Tel: (01635) 37715. Fax: (01635) 550230. Email: ieem@naturebureau.co.uk

The Institute of Wastes Management, 9 Saxon Court, St Peter's Gardens, Northampton NN1 1SX. Tel: (01604) 20426. Fax: (01604) 21339.

The Landscape Institute, 6-7 Barnard Mews, London SW1 1QU. Tel: (0171) 738 9166. Fax: (0171) 738 9134. Email: mail@l-i.org.uk Website: http://www.l-i.org.uk

Lantra, NAC, Kenilworth, Warwickshire CV8 2LG. Tel: (01203) 696996. Fax: (01203) 696732. Email: greentrain@dial.pipex.com Website: http://www.eto.co.uk

The National Trust, 36 Queen Anne's Gate, London SW1H 9AS. Tel: (0171) 222 9251. Fax: (0171) 222 5097. Careership office: Lanhydrock, Bodmin, Cornwall PL30 4DE. Tel: (01208) 74281. Fax: (01208) 77887.

The National Trust Volunteers Office, 33 Sheep Street, Cirencester, Glos GL7 1RQ. Tel: (01285) 651818.

Natural Environment Research Council, Polaris House, North Star Avenue, Swindon SN2 1EU. Tel: (01793) 411500. Fax: (01793) 411501.

Royal Town Planning Institute, 26 Portland Place, London W1N 4BE. Tel: (0171) 636 9107. Fax: (0171) 323 1582. Email: online@rtpi.org.uk Website: http://www.rtpi.org.uk

Scottish Conservation Projects Trust, Balallan House, 24 Allan Park,

Stirling FK8 2QG. Tel: (01786) 479697. Fax: (01786) 465359. Email: SCPT@dial.pipex.com

Scottish Natural Heritage, Personnel Section, 12 Hope Terrace, Edinburgh EH9 2AS. Tel: (0131) 447 4784. Fax: (0131) 446 2277.

Scottish Environment Protection Agency (SEPA), Head Office, Erskine Court, Castle Business Park, Stirling FK9 4TR. Tel: (01786) 457700. Fax: (01786) 446885. Email: info@sepa.org.uk Website: http://www.sepa.org.uk

Soil Association, Bristol House, 40-56 Victoria Street, Bristol BS1 6BY. Tel: (0117) 929 0661. Fax: (0117) 925 2504.

The Wildlife Trusts, The Green, Witham Park, Waterside South, Lincoln LN5 7JR. Tel: (01522) 544400. Fax: (01522) 511616. Email: wildlifersnc@cix.co.uk

World Wide Fund for Nature UK, Panda House, Weyside Park, Catteshall Lane, Godalming, Surrey GU7 1XR. Tel: (01483) 426444. Fax: (01483) 861006/426409. Website: http://www.wwf-uk.org

FURTHER AND HIGHER EDUCATION

ECCTIS 2000 Ltd, Oriel House, Oriel Road, Cheltenham, Glos GL50 1XP. Tel: (01242) 252627. Fax: (01242) 258600. Website: http://www.ecctis.co.uk Produces *UK Course Discover*.

UCAS, Fulton House, Jessop Avenue, Cheltenham, Glos GL50 3SH. Applicant enquiries: (01242) 227788. Website: http://www.ucas.ac.uk Produces *UCAS Handbook*.

GOVERNMENT OPPORTUNITIES

Environment & Heritage Agency for Northern Ireland, Countryside & Wildlife Branch, Calvert House, 23 Castle Place, Belfast BT1 1FY. Tel: (01232) 254754.

Local education authorities. Look in the telephone directory under the name of your local council.

Local Government Opportunities, Local Government Management Board, Layden House, 76-86 Turnmill Street, London EC1M 5QU. Tel: (0171) 296 6600. Fax: (0171) 296 6666. Careers website: http://www.datalake.com/lgo Recruitment website: http://www.datalake.com/lgo/jobsearch Produces careers information booklet '*catlog*'.

Training & Enterprise Councils (TECs)/Local Enterprise Councils (LECs). Look up in local telephone directory.

SPECIAL NEEDS

Skill, the National Bureau for Students with Disabilities, 336 Brixton Road, London SW9 7AA. Tel: (0171) 978 9890 (information service). Fax: (0171) 737 7479.

STUDENT FINANCE

Department for Education and Employment (England and Wales). Tel: (0800) 731 9133.

Department of Education for Northern Ireland, Rathgael House, Balloo Road, Bangor, Co Down BT18 7PR. Tel: (01247) 279279. Fax: (01247) 279100.

Student Awards Agency for Scotland, Gyleview House, 3 Redheughs Rigg, South Gyle, Edinburgh EH12 9HH. Tel: (0131) 244 5823. Fax: (0131) 244 5887.

Student Loans Company Ltd, 100 Bothwell Street, Glasgow G2 7JD. Tel: (0800) 405010 (freephone).

VOLUNTEERING

The National Centre for Volunteering, Regents Wharf, All Saints Street, London N1 9RL. Tel: (0171) 520 8900. Fax: (0171) 520 8910. Email: centrevol@aol.com

Voluntary Service Overseas (VSO), Enquiries Unit, 317 Putney Bridge Road, London SW15 2PN. Tel: (0181) 780 7500 (24 hours). Website: http://www.oneworld.org/vso/

LEARNING HOW TO LEARN MORE EFFECTIVELY

Buzan Centres Ltd, 54 Parkstone Road, Poole, Dorset BH15 2PX. Tel: (01202) 674676. Fax: (01202) 674776. Website: http://www. buzan.co.uk

Additional Resources

A selection of some of the various resources available. Many are obtainable for reference from libraries, schools, colleges, universities and careers centres.

CAREERS INFORMATION

Careers Encyclopaedia (Cassells, 1996).
catlog (Westlake Publishing Ltd, annual). Careers and training in local government.
CLIPS information leaflets (Lifetime Careers Wiltshire Ltd, annual). Available in most schools.
Environmental Careers Handbook (Trotman in association with the Institution of Environmental Sciences, 1995).
Occupations (COIC, annual).
The Penguin Careers Guide (Penguin, 1996).
PUSH Guide to Which University 1997 (McGraw-Hill Book Co, 1996). Also available on CD-ROM as PUSH-CD.
The Which? Guide to Choosing a Career Barbara Buffton (Which? Books Ltd, 1998).
Which? University on CD-ROM (Hobsons Publishing).
Who's Who in the Environment: England, Scotland, Wales. Available from the Environment Council.
Working in Environmental Services, Barbara Buffton (COIC, 1997).

FURTHER AND HIGHER EDUCATION

Degree Course Guide – Environmental Sciences (CRAC/Hobsons, annual).
Directory of Environmental Courses 1997-1999. A guide to academic, professional and vocational courses related to the environment. Available from the Environment Council.
Directory of Further Education (CRAC/Hobsons, annual).

Entrance Guide to Higher Education in Scotland (COSHEP, annual).
Higher Education and Disability: A guide to HE for people with disabilities (Hobsons/Skill, annual).
The Potter Guide to Higher Education (Dalebank Books, annual).
The Sixth Formers' Guide to Visiting Universities and Colleges (ISCO, annual).
Supporting Students in Higher Education (DfEE, free of charge by telephoning 0800 731 9133).
UK Course Discover database, (ECCTIS 2000 Ltd).
University and College Entrance – The official guide, (UCAS/Sheed & Ward, annual).
What do Graduates Do? (AGCAS with UCAS/CSU, annual).
Which Degree Series (four volumes, CRAC/Hobsons, annual).

FINANCIAL SUPPORT

The Directory of Grant Making Trusts, (Charities Aid Foundation).
The Educational Grants Directory, (The Directory of Social Change, 1996).
Financial Assistance for Students with Disabilities in Higher Education, (Skill, annual).
Financial Support for Students, (DfEE. Tel: (0800) 731 9133). This leaflet is for students in England and Wales; Scotland and Northern Ireland publish their own guides:- *Student Grants in Scotland; Grants and Loans to Students* (N. Ireland – Department of Education).
Sponsorship for Students, (CRAC/Hobsons, annual).
Students' Money Matters, (Trotman).
Tax Relief for Vocational Training, leaflet IR119. Available from any tax office or tax enquiry centre (address in telephone directory under Inland Revenue).

VOLUNTEERING

Green Volunteers – The world guide to voluntary work in nature conservation, edited by Fabio Ausenda, (Green Volunteers 1998, distributed by Vacation Work ISBN 88900167 1 X).
Worldwide Volunteering for Young People (1999 edition) – (How To Books in association with Youth for Britain).
Youth for Britain database: Worldwide Volunteering by Young People (Youth for Britain). Available from ECCTIS 2000 Ltd.

LEARNING HOW TO LEARN MORE EFFECTIVELY

The Mind Map Book – Radiant thinking, Tony Buzan, (BBC Publications, 1993).
Accelerated Learning, Colin Rose, (Dell New York, 1985).

MORE USEFUL WEBSITES

Information on the environment
http://www.environment.detr.gov.uk (website of The Department of the Environment, Transport and the Regions).
http://www/greenchannel.com

General information for young people on jobs, applications, careers, etc
http://www.thesite.org.uk

Job vacancies
http://www.jobsite.co.uk
http://www.Peoplebank.com
http://www.TheJob.com

MAGAZINES/JOURNALS

Earth Matters, available to members of Friends of the Earth.
EARTHlines, the newsletter of the Youth and Environment Network, available by subscription from the Council for Environmental Education.
Green Futures, 46 The Vineyard, Richmond, Surrey TW10 6AN. Tel: (0181) 948 0170. Fax: (0181) 948 6787. email: gf@candide. demon.co.uk
habitat – a digest of environmental news, campaigns and issues. Available on subscription (ten copies per year for £17.50) from the Environment Council.
Nature, English Nature.
New Scientist.
Ranger, a magazine available from the Countryside Management Association.

Index

USING THE INTERNET
How to make the most of the information superhighway

Graham Jones

Soon, nearly everyone in the developed world will have access to the Internet. This book shows you how and where to begin. Unlike other books on the 'Net', this down-to-earth practical guide, now in its second edition, will really help you to get onto the Net and start exploring the new 'information superhighway'. Using case examples, it illustrates some of the many benefits the Internet can bring, and the personal, business or educational goals you can achieve. Graham Jones is a leading business consultant and writer. He is the author of *How to Manage Computers at Work* in this series, and has contributed to many computer magazines. He runs his own publishing business that depends on the Internet for up-to-date information.

128pp. illus. 1 85703 237 3. 2nd edition.

BUYING A PERSONAL COMPUTER
How to choose the right equipment to meet your needs

Allen Brown

Many thousands of personal computers (PCs) are sold annually and they are becoming general purpose, everyday tools. Buying a PC for the first time represents a significant financial outlay. This book, now in a fully updated third edition, will help potential buyers in their choice of PC, their selection of peripherals, and appropriate software. It aims to be precise, yet with sufficient information to enable a new user to understand a PC specification and to ensure that it will be adequate for their needs. It will also provide information on applications that the buyer may be thinking of for the future. Dr Allen Brown is a Senior Lecturer in Electronics in the School of Applied Sciences at Anglia Polytechnic University, Cambridge.

176pp. illus. 1 85703 432 5. 3rd edition.

DOING VOLUNTARY WORK ABROAD
How to combine foreign travel with valuable work experience helping others

Mark Hempshell

Doing voluntary work abroad offers a great chance to combine foreign travel and valuable work experience, while helping others and learning about a different way of life. Here's the book that shows you the way – checking out the qualifications, skills and experience you may need, and finding the opportunities, whether in the UK or the rest of Europe, North and South America, or the countries of Africa and Asia. The book details the variety of opportunities available from working in conservation or technological development, to working with the disabled or other disadvantaged groups. Complete with typical case histories, and checklists of essential information about each type of assignment. Mark Hempshell is a specialist writer on international employment topics.

160pp. illus. 1 85703 469 4. 2nd edition.

WORKING WITH CHILDREN
How to find the right qualifications, training and job opportunities

Meg Jones

Working with children requires more than just a liking for babies. It requires application, dedication, commitment, the right attitudes, ability, and patience, as well as enjoying being with children. This book guides the reader through areas to be considered, opportunities available, variety of training attainable, and the long-term satisfaction of the work. Meg Jones has worked with children in a variety of capacities and settings over many years, and is frequently asked to advise on working with children. It is her belief that the greatest asset of childcare is the people working with the children. They must be the right people, able to gain appropriate quality experience and training. This book will help you decide if you could be one of those special people, and if so how to get there.

144pp. illus. 1 85703 340 X.

LEARNING NEW JOB SKILLS
How and where to obtain the right training to help you get on at work

Laurel Alexander

This book presents a positive approach to education and training and will enable you to make considered and informed choices about improving your job prospects. Taking a training course will improve your confidence, prepare you for a job with a future, potentially increase your earnings and bring fresh challenge back into your life. There are guidelines on how to get funding for training courses, getting vocational training if you are unemployed and returning to study as a mature student. Laurel Alexander is a specialist trainer and writer in career development and has helped hundreds of adults improve their working lives.

128pp. illus. 1 85703 375 2.

MAKING A WEDDING SPEECH
How to prepare and present a memorable speech

John Bowden

At thousands of weddings each year, many people are called on to 'say a few words'. But what do you say? How do you find the right words which will go down really well with the assembled company? Written by an experienced and qualified public speaker, this entertaining book shows you how to put together a simple but effective speech well suited to the particular occasion. Whether you are the best man, bridegroom, father of the bride or other participant, it will guide you every step from great opening lines to apt quotations, anecdotes, tips on using humour, and even contains 50 short model speeches you can use or adapt to any occasion.

166pp. 1 85703 347 7. 3rd edition.

HOW TO TRAVEL ROUND THE WORLD
Your practical guide to the experience of a lifetime

Nick Vandome

Written by a travel writer with extensive first-hand knowledge, this book explains: how to prepare for a real globetrotting adventure, how to plan your itinerary, how to organise passports, visa permits and other international paperwork, how to plan your means of travel, kitting yourself out, planning for health and safety on the move, learning to live with different languages and cultures, earning as you go, troubleshooting, and more.

224pp. illus. 1 85703 121 0.

WORKING IN COMPLEMENTARY THERAPIES
How to start a career in the new caring professions

Linda Wilson

Complementary medicine is a rapidly expanding field of employment which offers exciting new opportunities. Therapies such as massage, osteopathy and herbalism are gaining acceptance and recognition alongside orthodox medicine. Qualified practitioners can find openings in many different settings, including natural health centres and hospitals. This book examines the personal qualities needed to become a successful practitioner, guides you through the maze of therapies and training courses, and explains how to set up a practice. Linda Wilson began her career in complementary medicine in 1985. She is a member of the International Federation of Aromatherapists and is also trained in Reiki, Shen Tao acupressure and macrobiotics. She has her own practice in Devon and runs courses for adult education students and health professionals.

144pp. illus. 1 85703 352 3.

TAKING YOUR DRIVING TESTS
How to be prepared and feel confident of success

Angela Oatridge

Taking a driving test is perhaps one of the most stressful occasions in most people's lives. The purpose of this book is to help prepare the potential driving test candidate, so that he or she feels confident on the day. It also suggests how to cope when nerves and unexpected situations start to turn the big day into a nightmare. Angela Oatridge BSc (Hons) ADI, MIAM, has been a qualified driving instructor for nearly 30 years. She has run successful driving schools in England, Scotland and in Europe, and has also taught many people to become driving instructors. She is the author of *Teaching Someone to Drive* in this series.

112pp. illus. 1 85703 264 0.

PASSING THAT INTERVIEW
Your step-by-step guide to achieving success

Judith Johnstone

Using a systematic and practical approach, this book takes you step-by-step through the essential pre-interview groundwork, the interview encounter itself, and what you can learn from the experience. The book contains sample pre- and post-interview correspondence, and is complete with a guide to further reading, glossary of terms, and index. 'This is from the first class How To Books stable.' *Escape Committee Newsletter*. 'Offers a fresh approach to a well documented subject.' *Newscheck* (Careers Service Bulletin). 'A complete step-by-step guide.' *The Association of Business Executives*. Judith Johnstone is a Member of the Institute of Personnel & Development; she has been an instructor in Business Studies and adult literacy tutor, and has long experience of helping people at work.

144pp. illus. 1 85703 360 4. 4th edition.